The Art of Gifting: Using Free Offers to Win Customers' Hearts

SAM CHOO

Copyright © 2024 by Sam Choo.

All rights reserved.

No portion of this book may be reproduced in any form without written permission from the publisher or author.

https://www.facebook.com/samchooks/

Contents

Introduction: The Power of Generosity: Unlocking the Secrets of Free Gifts	1
Chapter 1: The Psychology of Giving: Why Free Gifts Matter	7
Chapter 2: The Benefits of Free: Boosting Sales, Loyalty, and Word-of-Mouth	15
Chapter 3: The Art of Selection: Choosing the Right Free Gifts	23
Chapter 4: The Science of Scarcity: Creating Urgency and Exclusivity	43
Chapter 5: The Power of Personalization: Tailoring Free Gifts to Your Audience	51
Chapter 6: Digital Delights: Leveraging E-books, Webinars, and Online Resources	59

Chapter 7: The Power of Ebooks: Creating Compelling Digital Reads — 69

Chapter 8: Crafting Captivating Online Courses — 89

Chapter 9: Webinars and Free Talks: Engaging Your Audience Live — 93

Chapter 10: Physical Pleasers: Leveraging Merchanise, Samples, Books, and Events to Wow — 99

Chapter 11: Experiential Extras: Creating Memorable Moments and Connections — 113

Chapter 12: Crafting Compelling Offers: Writing Copy that Converts — 123

Chapter 13: Delivering Delight: Ensuring a Seamless Customer Experience — 133

Chapter 14: Measuring Success: Tracking the Impact of Your Free Gifts — 145

Chapter 15: The Art of the Upsell: Turning Free Gifts into Profitable Relationships — 157

Conclusion: The Gift that Keeps on Giving: Sustaining a Culture of Generosity — 171

Introduction: The Power of Generosity: Unlocking the Secrets of Free Gifts

"The greatest good you can do for another is not just to share your riches but to reveal to him his own." - Benjamin Disraeli

1. The Trust Crisis in Modern Marketing

In today's digital age, consumers are inundated with marketing messages at every turn. From social media ads to email campaigns, from flashy website pop-ups to persistent remarketing, the average person encounters hundreds, if not thousands, of sales pitches daily. This constant barrage has led to what we might call a "trust crisis" in marketing.

Consider the landscape:

1. Scams and fraudulent offers abound, making consumers

wary of even legitimate opportunities.

2. Exaggerated claims and overhyped products have eroded consumer confidence.

3. The ease of setting up an online business has flooded the market with inexperienced or unscrupulous sellers.

4. Privacy concerns have made people hesitant to share their information.

As a result, potential customers approach new offers with skepticism and caution. They've been burned before, or they know someone who has. This skepticism creates a formidable barrier for honest businesses trying to connect with their audience.

The consequences of this trust crisis are severe:

- Sales pages often fail to convert, even when the product or service is excellent.

- Cold market outreach yields diminishing returns.

- Advertising costs increase as more touches are needed to build credibility.

- Businesses struggle to stand out in a sea of similar-looking offers.

The harsh reality is this: in today's market, **people buy you before they buy your product or service**. Without trust, even the most innovative product or life-changing service will struggle to find its audience.

This is the central challenge that this book aims to address. How can we, as ethical marketers and business owners, break through the wall of skepticism? **How can we build the trust** necessary to not just make a sale, but to create lasting, mutually beneficial relationships with our customers?

The answer lies in a counterintuitive approach: **giving before you get**. By offering genuine value upfront, without expectation of immediate return, we can begin to rebuild the bridge of trust between businesses and consumers.

In the following chapters, we'll explore how strategic giving—in the form of valuable free gifts—can be the key to overcoming the trust crisis. We'll delve into the psychology behind this approach, examine various strategies for implementation, and provide a roadmap for integrating this philosophy into your broader marketing efforts.

By the end of this book, you'll have a comprehensive understanding of how to use the art of giving to build trust, overcome skepticism, and create a loyal customer base in even the most challenging market conditions.

Now, I know what you might be thinking. "Free gifts? In this economy? Are you crazy?" Trust me, I get it. The idea of giving away valuable content or products for free might seem counterintuitive, especially when you're trying to grow your business. But here's the kicker – it works. And not just a little bit. We're talking game-changing, business-transforming results.

Take **Marie Forleo**, for example. You've probably heard of her, right? This powerhouse entrepreneur and life coach built her multi-million dollar empire on the foundation of free, valuable content. Her free YouTube series, "MarieTV," has attracted millions of viewers and turned countless fans into paying customers for her premium programs.

Or consider **Pat Flynn** of Smart Passive Income. He's famous for his "be everywhere" approach, which includes a ton of free content – from his blog posts to his podcast episodes. This strategy has helped him build a devoted following and a thriving business.

But don't worry – you don't need to be a Marie or a Pat to make this work. The beauty of the "free gift" strategy is that it's scalable. Whether you're just starting out or you're already making six figures, there's a way to make it work for you.

In this book, we're going to break it all down. We'll explore the psychology behind why free gifts are so powerful (spoiler alert: it's all about reciprocity). We'll dive into practical strategies for choosing the right gifts, creating a sense of urgency, and personalizing your offerings. And we'll get into the nitty-gritty tactics of how to create and deliver these gifts, whether they're digital downloads, physical products, or unforgettable experiences.

One area we'll focus on quite a bit is using books as lead generators. Why? Because books are incredible tools for establishing your expertise, providing value, and drawing potential customers into your world. And the best part? You don't need to write a 300-page tome to make this work. A well-crafted ebook can be just as effective – sometimes even more so.

Now, I know what some of you might be thinking. "This all sounds great, but I'm not a writer," or "I don't have time to create all this free content." Don't worry – we've got you covered. Throughout this book, we'll focus on simple, actionable strategies that you can implement right away, even if you're short on time or resources.

At the end of each chapter, you'll find a handy checklist and action items to help you put these ideas into practice. No fluff, no complications – just straightforward steps you can take to start seeing results.

So, are you ready to unlock the power of generosity in your business? Are you excited to discover how giving away valuable gifts can actually lead to more sales, more loyal customers, and a thriving business? Then let's dive in!

Remember, in the world of online business, the most successful entrepreneurs aren't always the ones who hold their cards closest to their chest. Often, they're the ones who are willing to give generously, trusting that what goes around, comes around. It's time to embrace the art of giving – and watch your business soar as a result.

Let's get started on this exciting journey together!

Action Items:

1. Reflect on your current lead generation strategy. Are you offering anything for free?

2. List 3-5 valuable pieces of content or resources you could potentially offer as a free gift.

3. Think about your ideal customer. What kind of free gift would they find irresistible?

Checklist for Getting Started:

[ ] Identify your primary business goal (e.g., grow email list, increase sales of a specific product)

[ ] Define your target audience clearly

[ ] Brainstorm potential free gift ideas

[ ] Evaluate your resources (time, skills, budget) for creating free gifts

[ ] Set a deadline for implementing your first free gift strategy

Chapter 1: The Psychology of Giving: Why Free Gifts Matter

"We make a living by what we get, but we make a life by what we give."
- Winston Churchill

Let's talk about something that might seem a bit counterintuitive at first: the power of giving stuff away for free. I know, I know – you're in business to make money, not give freebies. But stick with me here, because understanding the psychology behind free gifts can revolutionize your marketing strategy.

1. The Foundation of Free Gifts: Building Trust

At the heart of every successful marketing strategy lies a crucial element: trust. In today's skeptical market, where consumers are bombarded with countless sales pitches daily, building trust is more important—and more challenging—than ever.

This is where free gifts emerge as a powerful tool in your marketing arsenal. **The primary purpose of a free gift** isn't just to attract attention or generate leads—it's **to build trust.**

Why is trust so critical? Consider this: How often have you hesitated to make a purchase from an unfamiliar brand or individual? This hesitation is the trust barrier that causes many sales pages to fail. Potential customers, unfamiliar with you or your product, are naturally hesitant to part with their hard-earned money.

Free gifts break down this barrier. By offering something of genuine value without asking for anything in return (except perhaps an email address), you demonstrate:

1. **Expertise**: You show that you have knowledge or skills worth sharing.

2. **Confidence**: You're sure enough of your value to give some of it away for free.

3. **Generosity**: You're willing to help, even without immediate financial gain.

4. **Integrity**: You deliver real value, not just empty promises.

When you provide a free gift that truly helps your audience, you're not just giving away content or a product. You're offering a sample of your expertise, a taste of your quality, and a glimpse into the experience of being your customer. This builds the trust necessary for potential customers to consider your paid offerings.

As we explore the art of giving throughout this book, remember that at its core, every free gift is an opportunity to build trust. It's this trust that will ultimately drive your business growth, foster customer loyalty, and set the stage for long-term success.

2. The Reciprocity Principle: You Scratch My Back, I'll Scratch Yours

Let's start with a fundamental concept in human psychology: reciprocity. It's a fancy word for a simple idea – when someone does something nice for us, we feel compelled to return the favor.

Think about the last time a neighbor brought you a plate of cookies. Didn't you feel like you should do something nice for them in return? That's reciprocity in action.

In the business world, this principle is golden. When you offer a free gift to your potential customers, you're not just giving them a freebie – you're creating a sense of obligation. They'll feel inclined to reciprocate, often by engaging more with your content, signing up for your email list, or even making a purchase.

For example, digital marketing guru Neil Patel offers a free SEO analyzer tool on his website. Visitors get valuable insights about their website, and in return, they're more likely to explore Neil's paid services or products.

3. The Endowment Effect: We Value What We Own

Here's another psychological quirk that makes free gifts so powerful: the endowment effect. This principle states that people place a higher value on things they own compared to things they don't.

When you give someone a free gift, it becomes theirs. And suddenly, it's worth more to them than it was before they had it. This increased perceived value can extend to your brand as a whole.

Let's say you're a wellness coach and you offer a free ebook on "10 Simple Meditation Techniques for Busy Professionals." Once your potential client downloads this ebook, it becomes "their" meditation guide. They value it more because they own it, and by extension, they start to value your expertise more highly.

4. The Foot-in-the-Door Technique: Start Small, Go Big

Have you ever agreed to a small request, only to find yourself more willing to agree to a larger request later? That's the foot-in-the-door technique at work.

In marketing, free gifts act as that small initial request. When someone accepts your free offer, they're more likely to say yes to bigger commitments down the line.

For instance, life coach Tony Robbins often offers free content like motivational videos or short ebooks. People who consume this free content are more likely to attend his seminars or buy his products later on.

5. The Mere Exposure Effect: Familiarity Breeds Liking

Here's a fun fact: the more we're exposed to something, the more we tend to like it. This is called the mere exposure effect.

Free gifts give you more opportunities to expose potential customers to your brand. Each interaction, even if it's just with your free content, increases their familiarity and liking for your brand.

Take Marie Forleo's free content strategy. Her weekly MarieTV episodes expose viewers to her personality, style, and expertise regularly. Over time, viewers feel like they know Marie, making them more likely to invest in her B-School program when it's offered.

6. The IKEA Effect: We Value What We Create

Last but not least, let's talk about the IKEA effect. This principle suggests that people place a higher value on products they partially created themselves.

You can leverage this by offering free gifts that require some level of engagement or personalization from the recipient. For example, if you're a fitness coach, you might offer a free workout plan generator where clients input their goals and preferences to receive a customized plan.

7. Wrapping It Up

Understanding these psychological principles helps you see why free gifts are so powerful. They're not just freebies – they're strategic tools that tap into fundamental aspects of human behavior.

By offering valuable free gifts, you're not just being nice. You're triggering reciprocity, leveraging the endowment effect, getting your foot in the door, increasing exposure to your brand, and even engaging your audience in co-creation. All of these factors combine to make your free gifts a powerful tool for winning customers' hearts – and eventually, their business.

8. Action Items:

1. Identify one psychological principle from this chapter that resonates most with your business model.

2. Brainstorm a free gift idea that leverages this principle.

3. Think about how you can measure the impact of this psychological principle on your audience engagement.

9. Checklist:

[ ] Review your current free offerings and identify which psychological principles they leverage

[ ] Plan a new free gift that intentionally taps into one or more of these principles

[ ] Set up a system to track how recipients of your free gifts engage with your brand over time

[ ] Create a survey to ask your audience what types of free gifts they find most valuable

[ ] Analyze your competitors' free offerings and identify the psychological principles they're using

Remember, the key to success with free gifts is to always provide genuine value. These psychological principles work best when your free gift truly helps your audience. So, focus on creating gifts that your potential customers will love, and watch as the psychology of giving works its magic on your business growth!

Chapter 2: The Benefits of Free: Boosting Sales, Loyalty, and Word-of-Mouth

"The best things in life are free. The second-best things are very, very expensive." - Coco Chanel

Now that we've explored the psychology behind free gifts, let's talk about the tangible benefits they can bring to your business. Buckle up, because we're about to explore how giving away free stuff can actually boost your bottom line. Sounds crazy, right? But trust me, it works!

1. Supercharging Your Sales

Let's start with the big one – sales. You might be wondering, "How can giving stuff away for free possibly increase my sales?" Well, let me tell you, it's all about playing the long game.

Free gifts act as a powerful lead magnet. They draw potential customers into your world, giving them a taste of what you offer. It's like those free samples at the grocery store. You try a bite of that delicious cheese, and suddenly you're at the checkout with a whole block of it!

Take Pat Flynn of Smart Passive Income, for example. He offers a free ebook called "Ebooks the Smart Way." This free resource has brought countless readers to his site, many of whom go on to purchase his paid products or enroll in his courses.

The key here is to make sure your free gift showcases your expertise and leaves people wanting more. It should solve a problem for your audience, but also hint at the even greater value you can provide through your paid offerings.

2. Building Unshakeable Loyalty

Now, let's talk about loyalty. In today's competitive market, customer loyalty is worth its weight in gold. And guess what? Free gifts can help you build it.

When you provide value to someone without asking for anything in return, you start to build a relationship. You're no longer just a faceless brand – you're a helpful resource, a trusted advisor.

Consider the strategy of wellness guru Melissa Wood-Tepperberg. She regularly posts free workout videos on Instagram. These free resources have helped her build a devoted following who eagerly sign up for her paid app and longer programs.

Remember, loyal customers are not just more likely to buy from you repeatedly; they're also more likely to forgive the occasional mistake and stick with you through tough times.

3. Igniting Word-of-Mouth Marketing

Here's where things get really exciting. When you give away something truly valuable for free, people talk about it. And in the world of marketing, there's nothing more powerful than word-of-mouth.

Think about it. When was the last time you discovered an amazing free resource and kept it to yourself? Chances are, you told your friends, shared it on social media, or mentioned it in a conversation.

Digital marketer Neil Patel leverages this brilliantly with his free SEO analyzer tool. People use it, love it, and naturally share it with others in their network who could benefit from it. Each share expands Neil's reach without him spending an extra dime on advertising.

4. Establishing Authority and Trust

Free gifts, especially when they're packed with valuable information, help position you as an authority in your field. When you freely share your knowledge, you demonstrate confidence in your expertise.

Take Marie Forleo's free content strategy. Her MarieTV episodes cover a wide range of business and life topics, showcasing her expertise. This free content has helped establish her as a thought leader, making her paid B-School program an easy sell to her audience who already trust her advice.

5. Gathering Valuable Data and Insights

Here's a benefit that often gets overlooked: free gifts can help you gather valuable data about your audience. When someone signs up for your free ebook or webinar, you learn about their interests and needs.

For instance, if you're a fitness coach offering a free guide on "5 Effective Home Workouts," everyone who downloads it is telling you they're interested in home fitness. This information can help you tailor your future offerings and marketing messages.

6. Reducing Customer Acquisition Costs

Lastly, let's talk money – specifically, how free gifts can help you save it. Customer acquisition can be expensive, especially if you're relying heavily on paid advertising.

Free gifts, particularly digital ones like ebooks or webinars, can significantly reduce these costs. Once created, they can continue to attract new leads without ongoing expenses. It's like having a tireless salesperson working for you 24/7, drawing in potential customers while you sleep!

7. Wrapping It Up

So there you have it – the power of free in action. By strategically using free gifts, you can boost your sales, build customer loyalty, ignite word-of-mouth marketing, establish your authority, gather valuable data, and reduce your customer acquisition costs.

Remember, the key is to provide real value. Your free gift should be good enough that people would be willing to pay for it. That's how you create the kind of impact that translates into tangible business benefits.

8. Action Items:

1. Identify your most successful free offering. What makes it popular?

2. Plan a new free gift that addresses a specific pain point for your audience.

3. Set up a system to track how your free gifts impact your sales, customer loyalty, and word-of-mouth referrals.

9. Checklist:

[ ] Review your current sales funnel. Where could a free gift make the biggest impact?

[ ] Brainstorm ways to make your free gifts more shareable

[ ] Set up a feedback system to learn what your audience values most about your free offerings

[ ] Plan a campaign to re-engage past recipients of your free gifts

[ ] Analyze your customer acquisition costs. How could free gifts help reduce these?

Remember, in the world of online business, generosity can be your secret weapon. By giving freely, you're not losing out – you're investing in your business's growth and success. So go ahead, embrace the power of free, and watch your business soar!

Chapter 3: The Art of Selection: Choosing the Right Free Gifts

"Quality is never an accident; it is always the result of high intention, sincere effort, intelligent direction and skillful execution." - William A. Foster

Now that we understand why free gifts are so powerful, let's talk about how to choose the right ones. Because let's face it – not all free gifts are created equal. The right freebie can skyrocket your business, while the wrong one... well, let's just say it might not do much at all.

1. Introduction to the Importance of Free Gifts in Marketing

In today's competitive business landscape, capturing the attention of potential customers is more challenging than ever. However, even more crucial than gaining attention is building trust. This is where free gifts come into play as a powerful marketing tool. Far from being mere giveaways, strategically chosen free gifts can be the key to establishing trust and unlocking significant business growth.

Free gifts serve multiple crucial functions in modern marketing, with trust-building at the forefront:

- **Building Trust**: This is the primary and most vital function of a free gift. By providing value upfront without asking for anything in return, you demonstrate your expertise, reliability, and genuine interest in helping your audience. This builds the foundation of trust necessary for any business relationship.

- **Overcoming Sales Resistance**: Most sales pages fail because trust has not yet been established. A free gift allows potential customers to experience your value proposition without risk, reducing resistance to future purchases.

- **Lead Generation**: They entice potential customers to share their contact information, expanding your reach.

- **Showcasing Expertise**: Free gifts allow you to demonstrate your knowledge and capabilities, further reinforcing trust and positioning you as an authority in your field.

- **Customer Education**: They can help potential customers understand the value of your paid offerings, making them more receptive to future sales messages.

- **Differentiation**: In a crowded market, a well-chosen free gift can set you apart from competitors and create a positive first impression.

Remember, a free gift is often a potential customer's first experience with your brand. It's your chance to make a lasting impression, begin building a relationship based on trust, and lay the groundwork for future business success. In a world where consumers are increasingly skeptical of sales messages, a genuine, valuable free gift can be the key to breaking down barriers and fostering the trust necessary for successful sales.

2. Why Selection Matters

Choosing the right free gift is not a decision to be taken lightly. The gift you select can have far-reaching implications for your marketing efforts and overall business success.

Here's why the selection process is crucial:

- **First Impressions**: Your free gift often serves as an introduction to your brand. A poorly chosen gift can turn potential customers away, while the right one can create a positive, lasting impression.

- **Audience Alignment**: The right gift resonates with your target audience, addressing their needs and interests. A misaligned gift may attract the wrong audience or fail to engage your intended market.

- **Brand Representation**: Your free gift should reflect your brand's values, quality standards, and unique selling propositions. It's a tangible representation of what customers can expect from your paid offerings.

- **Resource Allocation**: Creating and distributing free gifts requires an investment of time and resources. Selecting the right gift ensures this investment generates optimal returns.

- **Conversion Potential**: A well-chosen gift naturally leads recipients towards your paid offerings, while a poorly selected one may fail to create this bridge.

By carefully selecting your free gift, you set the stage for successful lead nurturing, improved customer relationships, and ultimately, increased conversions and sales.

3. The Language of Free: Choosing the Right Term

In the world of marketing, there are numerous terms used to describe what we've been calling "free gifts." Each term carries its own connotations and may be more or less appropriate depending on your audience and brand image. Let's explore some common terms:

1. **Free Gift/Resource**: Straightforward and universally understood.

2. **Lead Magnet**: Common in digital marketing, but may not resonate with all audiences.

3. **Opt-in Offer**: Emphasizes the exchange of information for value.

4. **Freebie**: Casual and friendly, but may undervalue your offering.

5. **Bonus**: Suggests additional value on top of something else.

6. **Content Upgrade**: Specifically for enhancing existing content.

7. **Valuable Offer**: Emphasizes the worth of what you're providing.

8. **Complimentary Gift**: Adds a touch of class and generosity.

When choosing terminology, consider your audience and brand voice. For a broader audience, terms like "free resource" or "valuable offer" are more universally understood than industry-specific jargon like "lead magnet."

Avoid terms with negative connotations. For instance, "bait" or "tripwire" may make your audience feel like prey rather than valued customers. Remember, the goal is to build trust and provide genuine value.

To make the concept more relatable, consider using analogies familiar to your audience:

- "It's like a free sample at a grocery store."

- "Think of it as a free consultation with a professional."

- "It's similar to a free trial of a software product."

By carefully selecting your terminology, you can ensure your free gift is perceived as a genuine offer of value, setting the stage for a positive, trust-based relationship with your audience.

4. Types of Free Gifts

Free gifts come in various forms, each with its own strengths and ideal use cases. Understanding these types can help you choose the most effective option for your business:

a) **Digital Gifts:**

- E-books and PDF guides: In-depth resources on specific topics

- Webinars or video tutorials: Interactive learning experiences

- Templates or worksheets: Practical tools for immediate use

- Cheatsheets: Quick-reference guides with key information or steps

- Swipe files: Collections of proven, copyable content or formulas

- Resource lists: Curated collections of valuable tools, websites, or references

- Software trials or plugins: Hands-on experience with digital products

- Email courses: Delivered value over time, encouraging ongoing engagement

- Downloadable audio content: Podcasts or audio guides for on-the-go learning

- Infographics: Visual representations of complex information or data

- Digital calculators or interactive tools: Online utilities that provide personalized results

b) **Physical Gifts:**

- Product samples: Allow customers to try before they buy

- Branded merchandise: Practical items that keep your brand visible

- Print books or magazines: Tangible, high-perceived-value items

- Physical tools or accessories: Useful items related to your industry

c) **Experiential Gifts:**

- Free consultations: One-on-one interactions showcasing your expertise

- Trial memberships: Limited-time access to paid services

- Exclusive events or webinars: Special access fostering community

- Personalized assessments: Tailored insights demonstrating value

Each type of gift has its place in a marketing strategy. Digital gifts are easily scalable and distributed, physical gifts create a tangible connection, and experiential gifts offer unique, memorable interactions with your brand.

5. Finding Your Book's Golden Idea: Lessons from Bestselling Authors

When it comes to creating a compelling ebook or lead magnet, one of the biggest challenges is choosing the right topic. How do you know what will resonate with your audience and potentially lead to breakthrough success? Sometimes, the answer lies in unexpected places. Many of today's bestselling authors stumbled upon their most successful ideas through blog posts, personal experiences, or professional insights that struck a chord with their audience. Let's explore some inspiring examples of how renowned authors discovered the topics that launched their careers. These stories not only provide valuable insights but also demonstrate that your next big idea might be hiding in plain sight - perhaps in your most popular blog post, a personal experience, or a unique perspective you take for granted.

Examples of how writers found their breakthrough subjects.

1: Mark Manson - "The Subtle Art of Not Giving a F*ck"

His blog post titled "The Subtle Art of Not Giving a F*ck" went viral, receiving millions of views. Recognizing the post's popularity, Manson expanded on the concept, turning it into a full-length book with the same title. The book became a #1 New York Times bestseller and has sold over 12 million copies worldwide. This success stemmed from Manson's ability to recognize the resonance of his message with readers and expand it into a comprehensive philosophy for life.

2: Ryan Holiday - "The Obstacle Is the Way"

While working as a marketing director for American Apparel, Holiday wrote a blog post about Stoicism and how it applied to modern life. The post gained significant traction, leading Holiday to delve deeper into the subject. This exploration resulted in his book "The Obstacle Is the Way," which popularized Stoic philosophy for a contemporary audience. The book's success established Holiday as a leading voice on Stoicism and personal development.

3: Elizabeth Gilbert - "Eat, Pray, Love"

Gilbert's memoir began as a personal journey to recover from a difficult divorce. She took a year-long trip to Italy, India, and Indonesia, documenting her experiences. Initially, she had no intention of writing a book about it. However, as she shared her stories with friends, she realized there was significant interest in her journey of self-discovery. The resulting book became an international bestseller and was adapted into a successful film.

4: Malcolm Gladwell - "The Tipping Point"

Gladwell's journey to becoming a bestselling author started with an article he wrote for The New Yorker about the sudden drop in crime in New York City. The article explored the concept of social epidemics and how small changes can have big effects. The overwhelming response to this article led Gladwell to expand on the idea, resulting in his first book, "The Tipping Point," which became a global phenomenon and launched his career as a popular science writer.

5: Marie Kondo - "The Life-Changing Magic of Tidying Up"

Kondo's journey began when she was a college student in Tokyo, organizing friends' closets as a side job. She developed her own tidying method and started a waiting list for her services. A publisher approached her about writing a book after hearing about her unique approach. The resulting book became an international bestseller, spawning a global decluttering movement and a Netflix series.

6: Tim Ferriss - "The 4-Hour Workweek"

Ferriss's breakthrough came from his own experiments in lifestyle design and productivity. He initially gave a lecture at Princeton University about his methods for reducing workload while increasing output. The lecture was so popular that he decided to turn it into a book proposal. After being rejected by 26 publishers, the book was finally accepted and went on to become a massive bestseller, launching Ferriss's career as an author and podcaster.

These stories highlight a common thread: many successful authors find their breakthrough topics by paying attention to what resonates with their audience, whether it's through blog posts, personal experiences, or professional insights. They then have the insight to expand these ideas into full-length books, often tapping into broader themes or needs that weren't being adequately addressed in the existing literature.

6. Criteria for Selecting the Right Free Gift

Choosing the perfect free gift involves considering several key factors:

a) **Relevance to Your Audience**:

- Does it address a specific pain point or desire of your target market?

- Is it something your audience would actively seek out or find valuable?

b) **Alignment with Your Brand and Offerings**:

- Does the gift reflect your brand's quality and values?

- Does it naturally lead into your paid products or services?

c) **Perceived Value vs. Cost to Produce**:

- Does the perceived value of the gift exceed its production cost?
- Can you create something high-value without breaking the bank?

d) **Ease of Delivery and Consumption**:

- Can you distribute the gift efficiently to your audience?
- Is it easy for recipients to access and use the gift?

e) **Uniqueness and Differentiation**:

- Does your gift stand out from what competitors are offering?
- Does it showcase your unique expertise or approach?

f) **Scalability**:

- Can you offer this gift to a growing audience without significant additional costs?

g) **Measurability**:

- Can you track the performance and ROI of this gift?

h) **Timeliness and Relevance:**

- Is the gift evergreen, or does it address current trends or concerns?

By carefully considering these criteria, you can select a free gift that not only attracts potential customers but also effectively supports your broader marketing and business goals.

7. Know Your Audience Inside and Out

First things first – you need to know your audience like the back of your hand. What keeps them up at night? What are their biggest challenges? What kind of solutions are they desperately searching for?

For example, if you're a wellness coach targeting busy professionals, they might be struggling with stress management or finding time for self-care. A free guide on "5-Minute Meditation Techniques for the Office" could be just what they need.

Remember, the goal is to provide something so valuable that your audience thinks, "I can't believe this is free!"

8. Align with Your Paid Offerings

Here's a pro tip: your free gift should be a natural stepping stone to your paid products or services. Think of it as a "taste test" that leaves them hungry for more.

Take bestselling author and writing coach Joanna Penn. She offers a free author blueprint that gives aspiring authors a taste of her expertise. This free gift naturally leads into her paid courses and books on writing and publishing.

When selecting your free gift, ask yourself: "How does this pave the way for my paid offerings?"

9. Consider Different Formats

Free gifts come in all shapes and sizes. Here are some popular options:

1. Ebooks or PDF guides

2. Video tutorials or mini-courses

3. Webinars or workshops

4. Templates or worksheets

5. Free trials of your product or service

6. Podcasts or audio guides

7. Quizzes or assessments

The key is to choose a format that:

a) Your audience prefers

b) Showcases your strengths

c) Delivers value efficiently

For instance, if you're a charismatic speaker, a video series might work better than a written guide. If your audience is always on the go, maybe an audio guide or podcast would be more appealing.

10. Make It Actionable

The best free gifts don't just provide information – they inspire action. Your audience should be able to implement what they've learned and see results quickly.

Digital marketer Ryan Deiss does this well with his "Customer Avatar Worksheet." It's a free, fillable PDF that helps businesses define their ideal customer. It's practical, actionable, and provides immediate value.

When creating your free gift, ask yourself: "What quick win can I give my audience?"

11. Keep It Focused

It's tempting to pack your free gift with everything you know. Resist that urge! A focused, specific gift is often more valuable than a broad, general one.

For example, instead of a general "Guide to Social Media Marketing," you might offer "10 Proven Instagram Strategies to Double Your Followers in 30 Days."

The more specific and focused your free gift, the more likely it is to attract your ideal customers.

12. Make It Easily Consumable

In our fast-paced world, attention spans are short. Your free gift should be easily consumable. This doesn't mean it can't be comprehensive, but it should be structured in a way that's easy to digest.

Consider how productivity guru David Allen offers a free PDF of his "Getting Things Done Workflow Map." It's a one-page visual guide that distills his entire productivity system into an easy-to-grasp format.

13. Test and Refine

Choosing the right free gift is often a process of trial and error. Don't be afraid to experiment with different options and see what resonates most with your audience.

Use analytics to track which free gifts get the most downloads or sign-ups. Pay attention to feedback from your audience. What do they love? What do they wish was included?

Renowned marketer Seth Godin is known for constantly experimenting with his free offerings, from ebooks to online courses to his daily blog. This approach allows him to continually refine his strategy and provide maximum value to his audience.

14. Keep It Fresh

Lastly, don't forget to keep your free gifts updated. As your industry evolves and your audience's needs change, your free offerings should evolve too.

For instance, social media expert Mari Smith regularly updates her free resources to reflect the latest changes in Facebook's algorithms and features.

15. Wrapping It Up

Choosing the right free gift is both an art and a science. It requires a deep understanding of your audience, a clear alignment with your business goals, and a willingness to experiment and refine.

Remember, the best free gifts are those that provide genuine value, showcase your expertise, and leave your audience eager to engage more deeply with your brand. Get this right, and you'll have a powerful tool for growing your business and making a real impact in your customers' lives.

16. Action Items:

1. Conduct a survey to understand what type of free gift your audience would find most valuable.

2. Brainstorm 3-5 ideas for free gifts that align with your paid offerings.

3. Choose one idea and create an outline or rough draft of your free gift.

17. Checklist:

[ ] Define your ideal customer avatar in detail

[ ] List the top 3 problems your audience is trying to solve

[ ] Evaluate your current free offerings – are they still relevant and valuable?

[ ] Research what free gifts your competitors are offering

[ ] Decide on a format for your new free gift (e.g., ebook, video, template)

[ ] Set up a system to gather feedback on your free gift

[ ] Plan how you'll promote your new free gift

Remember, the right free gift can be a game-changer for your business. It's worth investing time and effort to get it right. So go ahead, start brainstorming, and create something your audience will absolutely love!

Chapter 4: The Science of Scarcity: Creating Urgency and Exclusivity

"The way to love anything is to realize that it may be lost." - G.K. Chesterton

We've talked about the power of free gifts, but now let's explore how to make those freebies even more irresistible. Enter the science of scarcity – a powerful psychological trigger that can supercharge your free gift strategy.

1. The FOMO Factor

Let's start with a concept we're all familiar with: FOMO, or the Fear of Missing Out. It's that nagging feeling that if we don't act now, we might lose out on something great. And guess what? It's a marketer's secret weapon.

When you apply scarcity to your free gifts, you tap into this primal fear. Suddenly, your audience isn't just thinking, "Oh, that's nice." They're thinking, "I need to get this NOW before it's gone!"

2. Limited Time Offers

One of the simplest ways to create scarcity is through limited-time offers. Think about those countdown timers you see on sales pages. They're not just for show – they work!

For example, digital marketing expert Amy Porterfield often offers her free webinars for a limited time. When people know they only have 48 hours to watch, they're much more likely to make time for it.

You could try something like: "Download my free 'Instagram Growth Hacks' ebook – available for the next 72 hours only!"

3. Limited Quantity

Another effective scarcity tactic is to limit the quantity of your free gift. This works especially well for higher-value freebies or physical products.

Fitness guru Kayla Itsines has used this strategy by offering a limited number of free workout plans to the first X number of subscribers.

This not only creates urgency but also makes the recipients feel special for being "chosen."

Try something like: "The first 100 people to sign up will receive a free 30-minute consultation call!"

4. Exclusive Access

People love feeling like they're part of an exclusive group. You can leverage this by offering your free gift as part of a "members-only" deal.

For instance, entrepreneur Russell Brunson offers free access to some of his training videos, but only to members of his free "Funnel Hackers" community. This not only makes the free content feel more valuable but also encourages people to join his community.

You might say: "Join our free 'Marketing Masterminds' Facebook group for exclusive access to weekly training videos!"

5. The Power of 'By Invitation Only'

Want to really ramp up the exclusivity factor? Make your free gift available by invitation only. This tactic makes people feel specially chosen and valued.

High-end coach Tony Robbins sometimes uses this approach, offering free tickets to his events to a select group of people. Even though it's free, the "invite-only" status makes it feel incredibly valuable.

Try: "You've been specially selected to receive our free 'Advanced SEO Tactics' video course. Click here to accept your invitation!"

6. Seasonal or Event-Based Scarcity

Tying your free offer to a specific season or event can create natural scarcity. People understand that holiday deals or birthday specials won't last forever.

Wellness coach Gabby Bernstein often offers free meditations or journal prompts tied to events like New Year's or the summer solstice. The seasonal nature of these gifts creates built-in urgency.

Example: "Grab our free 'Summer Body Workout Plan' – available only until June 30th!"

7. The Scarcity Paradox

Here's an interesting twist – sometimes, making something scarce can actually increase its perceived abundance. How? When people see others clamoring for a limited resource, they assume it must be valuable and abundant in quality, if not quantity.

This is why you often see marketers saying things like, "Due to overwhelming demand, we've opened up 50 more spots for our free webinar!" It signals both scarcity (limited spots) and abundance (high demand).

8. Ethical Considerations

Now, a word of caution. While scarcity is a powerful tool, it's crucial to use it ethically. Never create fake scarcity – if you say there are only 100 spots available, there should really only be 100 spots. Your audience can smell inauthenticity a mile away, and it can seriously damage your credibility.

9. Balancing Act

Remember, the goal is to create a sense of urgency and exclusivity, not to stress people out. Balance your scarcity tactics with reassurance about the value you're offering.

For instance, you might say: "This free guide is only available for the next 24 hours. But don't worry – it's packed with actionable tips you can start using right away to grow your business!"

10. Wrapping It Up

Scarcity can be a game-changer when it comes to your free gifts. By creating a sense of urgency and exclusivity, you can dramatically increase the perceived value of your offerings and motivate your audience to take action.

Whether you're using limited-time offers, exclusive access, or invitation-only gifts, the key is to be genuine, ethical, and always focused on providing real value to your audience.

11. Action Items:

1. Choose one of your existing free gifts and brainstorm how you could add an element of scarcity to it.

2. Plan a limited-time offer for a new free gift and map out your promotion strategy.

3. Experiment with different scarcity tactics and track which ones resonate most with your audience.

12. Checklist:

[ ] Review your current free offerings – are there opportunities to introduce scarcity?

[ ] Decide on a scarcity tactic to try (e.g., limited time, limited quantity, exclusive access)

[ ] Create compelling copy that emphasizes the scarcity of your offer

[ ] Set up systems to ensure you can deliver on your scarcity claims (e.g., automated email sequences, countdown timers)

[ ] Plan how you'll follow up with people who claim your scarce free gift

[ ] Prepare a strategy for what happens after the scarcity period ends

Remember, scarcity is a powerful tool, but it's not about tricking people – it's about motivating them to take advantage of the genuine value you're offering. Use it wisely, and watch as your free gifts become irresistible to your audience!

Chapter 5: The Power of Personalization: Tailoring Free Gifts to Your Audience

"The more you engage with customers the clearer things become and the easier it is to determine what you should be doing." - John Russell

We've covered a lot of ground so far, but now it's time to talk about one of the most powerful strategies in your free gift arsenal: **personalization**. In today's world of information overload, a personalized approach can make your free gift stand out like a lighthouse in a fog. Let's explore how to make your audience feel like your free gift was made just for them.

1. The Personal Touch in a Digital World

In our increasingly digital world, people crave personal connections more than ever. When you tailor your free gifts to your audience's specific needs and preferences, you're not just offering value – you're building a relationship.

Think about it. How do you feel when you receive a birthday card that's clearly a generic message versus one that mentions your specific interests or shared memories? The personalized one means more, right? The same principle applies to your free gifts.

2. Segmentation: The Foundation of Personalization

Before you can personalize, you need to understand the different segments of your audience. Not all your followers have the same needs or interests.

For example, let's say you're a fitness coach. Your audience might include:

- Beginners just starting their fitness journey

- Intermediate exercisers looking to step up their game

- Advanced fitness enthusiasts seeking specialized knowledge

Each of these groups would benefit from different types of free gifts. A "5 Simple Exercises for Beginners" guide would be perfect for the first group but might not excite the advanced crowd.

3. Gathering Data: The Key to Effective Personalization

To personalize effectively, you need data. But don't worry – you don't need to become a data scientist. Here are some simple ways to gather information:

1. **Surveys**: Ask your audience directly about their needs and preferences.

2. **Quizzes**: Create fun, interactive quizzes that provide value to your audience while gathering information.

3. **Email Segmentation**: Use your email marketing tool to track which content subscribers engage with most.

4. **Social Media Insights**: Pay attention to which posts get the most engagement from your followers.

Digital marketer Ryan Levesque has built an entire business around his "Ask Method," which uses quizzes to segment audiences and provide personalized recommendations.

4. Types of Personalization

Now, let's look at different ways you can personalize your free gifts:

Content Personalization

Tailor the content of your free gift based on your audience's interests or needs. For instance, if you're a travel blogger, you might offer different city guides based on whether someone is interested in budget travel, luxury experiences, or family-friendly activities.

Format Personalization

Some people prefer reading, others like videos, and some learn best through interactive content. Offer your free gift in multiple formats to cater to different learning styles.

Timing Personalization

Send your free gift at the right time. If you know a subscriber's birthday or anniversary, that could be a perfect time to offer a special free gift.

Name Personalization

It's simple, but effective. Using a person's name in your free gift (like "Sarah's Personal Productivity Plan") can make it feel more special.

Industry-Specific Personalization

If you serve multiple industries, create versions of your free gift tailored to each one. A "Marketing Guide for Dentists" will resonate more with dentists than a general marketing guide.

Personalization in Action

Let's look at some examples of effective personalization:

- Fitness app MyFitnessPal offers personalized meal plans as a free gift, based on the user's dietary preferences and fitness goals.

- Copywriting expert Joanna Wiebe of Copyhackers offers different free email courses based on whether you're a beginner or experienced copywriter.

- Meditation app Headspace personalizes the user experience by asking about meditation experience and goals, then recommending specific free meditations.

6. The Power of Progressive Personalization

Remember, personalization doesn't have to happen all at once. You can use a strategy called progressive personalization, where you gradually collect more information and refine your personalization over time.

For example, you might start by offering a general free ebook to everyone. Based on which chapters they spend the most time on, you could then offer more specialized free resources in those areas of interest.

7. Avoiding the Creepy Factor

While personalization is powerful, it's important not to overdo it. There's a fine line between "Wow, this is perfect for me!" and "Uh, how do they know so much about me?"

Always be transparent about how you're using people's data, and give them control over their information. And remember, the goal is to be helpful, not invasive.

8. Wrapping It Up

Personalization can transform your free gifts from generic offerings to invaluable resources that speak directly to each segment of your audience. By tailoring your free gifts, you're not just providing more value – you're building stronger connections with your audience and setting the stage for long-term relationships.

9. Action Items:

- Identify 2-3 distinct segments within your audience.

- Create a simple survey to learn more about your audience's preferences.

- Plan a personalized free gift for one of your audience segments.

10. Checklist:

[ ] Review your current audience data – what do you already know about your followers?

[ ] Set up a system for collecting more detailed audience information

[ ] Brainstorm ways to personalize your existing free gifts for different audience segments

[ ] Plan a personalized email sequence to deliver your free gift

[ ] Test different levels of personalization and track the results

[ ] Ensure you have a clear privacy policy explaining how you use audience data

Remember, personalization is about making your audience feel seen and understood. When you get it right, your free gifts won't just be appreciated – they'll be cherished. So go ahead, get personal, and watch your audience engagement soar!

Chapter 6: Digital Delights: Leveraging E-books, Webinars, and Online Resources

"Content is fire, social media is gasoline." - Jay Baer

In this chapter, we're going to explore the wonderful world of digital freebies. These virtual goodies are the bread and butter of modern marketing, offering endless possibilities to showcase your expertise and provide value to your audience. Let's dive in and discover how to create digital delights that your audience will love!

1. The Power of Digital

Before we jump into specific types of digital freebies, let's talk about why they're so powerful:

- **Scalability**: Once created, digital resources can be distributed to an unlimited number of people at virtually no extra cost.

- **Accessibility**: Your audience can access digital freebies anytime, anywhere.

- **Updatability**: You can easily update and improve digital resources as needed.

- **Trackability**: It's easy to measure engagement and gather data with digital freebies.

Now, let's explore some of the most effective types of digital freebies:

2. E-books: The Classic Digital Freebie

E-books are a fantastic way to provide in-depth value to your audience. They allow you to dive deep into a topic and showcase your expertise.

Tips for creating compelling e-books:

- Choose a specific, targeted topic
- Use an attention-grabbing title
- Include actionable tips and strategies
- Make it visually appealing with graphics and formatting

- Keep it concise – aim for 15-30 pages

For example, marketing guru Neil Patel offers a free e-book called "The Advanced Guide to Content Marketing." It's comprehensive, actionable, and perfectly aligned with his paid services.

3. Webinars: Interactive Learning Experiences

Webinars offer a unique opportunity to engage with your audience in real-time. They're perfect for demonstrating processes, answering questions, and building personal connections.

Keys to successful webinars:

- Choose a topic that addresses a specific pain point

- Promote your webinar well in advance

- Prepare engaging visuals and examples

- Include interactive elements like Q&A sessions

- Offer a special deal or exclusive content to live attendees

Marie Forleo, for instance, often uses free webinars to provide value and promote her B-School program. Her webinars are engaging, packed with actionable advice, and always leave the audience wanting more.

4. Online Courses: In-Depth Learning

While full courses are often premium products, mini-courses can make excellent free gifts. They provide structured learning experiences that can really showcase your teaching style.

Tips for creating mini-courses:

- Break your content into easily digestible modules
- Include a mix of video, text, and interactive elements
- Provide actionable assignments or worksheets
- Create a clear learning path with defined outcomes
- Use the course as a teaser for more comprehensive paid offerings

Fitness expert Kayla Itsines offers a free 7-day trial of her workout app, which is essentially a mini-course in her fitness methodology. It's a perfect taste of her paid program.

5. Checklists and Templates: Quick Wins

Sometimes, the most valuable freebies are the simplest. Checklists and templates offer immediate utility and quick wins for your audience.

Ideas for effective checklists and templates:

- Social media content calendars
- Project management templates
- Goal-setting worksheets
- Industry-specific checklists (e.g., "10-Point SEO Audit Checklist")
- Email templates for common business scenarios

For example, productivity guru David Allen offers a free PDF of his "Getting Things Done" workflow diagram – a simple but powerful tool from his popular methodology.

6. Video Tutorials: Show, Don't Just Tell

Video tutorials can be incredibly effective, especially for demonstrating processes or techniques. They allow your audience to see your personality and teaching style.

Tips for creating engaging video tutorials:

- Keep them short and focused – aim for 5-15 minutes
- Use screen recording software for tech-related tutorials
- Ensure good lighting and audio quality

- Include a clear call-to-action at the end

- Optimize your video titles and descriptions for search

Pat Flynn of Smart Passive Income offers numerous free video tutorials on his YouTube channel, covering everything from podcast setup to email marketing strategies.

7. Podcasts: Audio Learning on the Go

While ongoing podcasts require significant commitment, single podcast episodes or short series can make great free gifts. They're perfect for audiences who prefer audio content.

Ideas for podcast-style freebies:

- Interview series with industry experts

- Deep dives into specific topics

- Behind-the-scenes looks at your business processes

- Q&A sessions addressing common audience questions

- Case studies or success stories

Tim Ferriss occasionally offers free podcast episodes that aren't part of his regular show, providing extra value to his audience.

8. Interactive Tools: Engagement Boosters

Interactive tools like quizzes, calculators, or assessments can provide personalized value to your audience while also gathering valuable data.

Examples of interactive tools:

- Personal brand quiz
- ROI calculator
- Fitness level assessment
- Career path finder
- Personality type indicator

HubSpot offers a free Website Grader tool that analyzes websites and provides personalized improvement suggestions – a perfect lead-in to their paid services.

9. Wrapping It Up

Digital freebies offer endless possibilities to provide value, showcase your expertise, and attract your ideal audience. The key is to choose the format that best suits your content, your skills, and your audience's preferences.

Remember, the goal isn't just to create a freebie – it's to create a valuable resource that solves a problem for your audience and leaves them eager to engage more deeply with your brand.

10. Action Items:

- Identify your top three areas of expertise that could be turned into digital freebies.
- Choose one digital freebie format and outline your content.
- Set a deadline for creating your first (or next) digital freebie.

11. Checklist:

[ ] Assess your current digital freebies – are they still relevant and valuable?

[ ] Research which types of digital content your audience engages with most

[ ] Plan the creation process for your chosen digital freebie

[ ] Set up a system to deliver your digital freebie (e.g., email autoresponder, landing page)

[ ] Create a promotion plan for your new digital freebie

[ ] Establish metrics to measure the success of your digital freebie

Remember, the digital world is your oyster when it comes to free gifts. Get creative, focus on providing genuine value, and don't be afraid to experiment with different formats. Your perfect digital delight is waiting to be created!

Chapter 7: The Power of Ebooks: Creating Compelling Digital Reads

"A book is a gift you can open again and again." - Garrison Keillor

In this chapter, we're diving deep into the world of ebooks - one of the most versatile and powerful free gifts in your digital marketing toolkit.

1. Why Ebooks?

Ebooks allow you to:

- Showcase your expertise in-depth
- Provide tangible value to your audience
- Establish authority in your niche

- Capture leads effectively

2. Rules for Creating an Effective Ebook Lead Magnet

When crafting an ebook to serve as a lead magnet, it's crucial to follow certain rules to maximize its effectiveness. These guidelines will help ensure your ebook provides value to your audience while also serving your marketing goals.

Rule 1: Focus on One Specific Problem

Your ebook should address a single, well-defined problem—ideally, the most pressing issue your target audience faces. By concentrating on one problem, you can:

- Provide in-depth, actionable information

- Position yourself as an expert on that specific issue

- Attract highly qualified leads who are actively seeking a solution to that problem

Rule 2: Keep It Concise and Digestible

Aim for a length of 1,500 to 2,500 words, which typically takes 5 to 10 minutes to read. This approach:

- Respects your readers' time

- Increases the likelihood that they'll read the entire ebook

- Leaves them wanting more, setting the stage for your upsell

Rule 3: Deliver a Substantial Portion of the Solution

Your ebook should provide a significant part of the solution, often described as the 'what' and 'why'. This is commonly referred to as the "50% rule," but the exact percentage can vary. Here's what you need to know:

- **The 50-50 Approach**: Many marketers aim to provide about half of the solution in the lead magnet, leaving the other half for the paid offer.

- **Flexibility in Percentages**: Some prefer a 40-60 split or other ratios. The exact numbers aren't as important as the underlying principle.

Here's what really matters:

1. **Substantial Value in the Lead Magnet**: Your free offer should provide enough value that the reader feels they've gained something significant, even if they never make a purchase.

2. **Clear Need for More**: At the same time, your lead magnet should clearly indicate that there's more to learn or gain, creating a natural desire for your paid offer.

3. **Logical Progression**: The transition from free to paid content should feel natural and necessary for those who want to fully solve their problem or achieve their goal.

4. **Ethical Balance**: You're aiming to give enough to be genuinely helpful, while also running a sustainable business through your paid offerings.

Whether you think of it as 50-50, 40-60, or some other split, the fundamental idea remains the same: provide real value upfront, while clearly demonstrating the additional value of your paid offer.

This approach:

- Offers genuine value, building trust and credibility

- Creates a knowledge foundation for your readers

- Generates curiosity about the complete solution

- Sets the stage for your upsell by demonstrating the value of your expertise

Rule 4: Lead to Your Upsell

Design your ebook to naturally lead into your paid offering, which will reveal the 'how' of the solution. For example:

- Ebook: "5 Essential Supplements for Optimal Health" (what to take and why)

- Upsell: "The Complete Guide to Supplement Timing and Dosage" (how to take them)

Rule 5: Create a Compelling Title

Your ebook's title is crucial - it's often the first (and sometimes only) thing potential readers see. A compelling title can dramatically increase the chances of your ebook being downloaded and read. Here are some effective templates for creating titles that grab attention:

1: The Step-by-Step Promise

Template: "[X] Steps to [Desirable Outcome] Without [Common Pain Point] in [Time Frame]"

Examples:

- "5 Steps to a Thriving Online Business Without Working 80-Hour Weeks in Just 30 Days"

- "3 Steps to Flawless Skin Without Expensive Treatments in

Just 2 Weeks"

2: The Insider Secrets

Template: "[X] Secrets [Experts/Pros] Don't Want You To Know About [Topic]"

Examples:

- "7 Secrets Top Chefs Don't Want You To Know About Perfect Pastry"

- "12 Secrets Wall Street Insiders Don't Want You To Know About Investing"

3: The Multiplier

Template: "[X]X Your [Desirable Outcome] With These [Y] [Strategies/Tips/Hacks]"

Examples:

- "10X Your Productivity With These 5 Simple Hacks"

- "5X Your Social Media Engagement With These 3 Counterintuitive Strategies"

4: The Efficiency Promise

Template: "[X] Your [Goal] at [50-70%] Less [Time/Money/Effort]" **Examples**:

- "Double Your Savings at 50% Less Effort: The Smart Budgeter's Guide"

- "Triple Your Website Traffic at 70% Less Cost: The Lean SEO Playbook"

5: The Curiosity Gap

Template: "The [Unexpected Number] [Things/Ways/Tricks] That [Surprising Outcome]"

Examples:

- "The 3 Unconventional Habits That Transformed My Career Overnight"

- "The 7 Counterintuitive Tricks That Helped Me Lose 30 Pounds in 60 Days"

6: The How-To Hook

Template: "How to [Achieve Desirable Outcome] Even If [Common Obstacle]"

Examples:

- "How to Launch a Successful Side Hustle Even If You're Working Full-Time"

- "How to Master a New Language Even If You Struggled in

School"

7: The Question Trigger

Template: "Are You Making These [X] [Topic] Mistakes?"

Examples:

- "Are You Making These 5 Fatal Email Marketing Mistakes?"
- "Are You Committing These 7 Deadly Sins of Personal Finance?"

8: The Urgent Call

Template: "[X] [Things/Ways] to [Achieve Goal] Before [Deadline/Event]" **Examples**:

- "9 Ways to Boost Your Immune System Before Flu Season Hits"
- "5 Things You Must Do to Protect Your Assets Before the New Tax Law Takes Effect"

When crafting your title, keep these tips in mind:

1. **Use numbers**: Odd numbers often perform better than even numbers.

2. **Include power words**: Words like "secrets," "insider,"

"proven," or "essential" can increase appeal.

3. **Address pain points**: Mention common challenges your audience faces.

4. **Promise a benefit**: Clearly state what the reader will gain.

5. **Create urgency**: Use time-related words to encourage immediate action.

6. **Be specific**: The more precise your title, the more it will resonate with your target audience.

Remember, your title should accurately reflect the content of your ebook. While it's important to be attention-grabbing, it's equally crucial to deliver on the promise your title makes. A compelling title combined with valuable content is the key to a successful lead magnet ebook.

Rule 6: Incorporate Visual Elements

Use charts, infographics, or images to break up text and illustrate key points. This enhances readability and information retention.

Rule 7: Include a Clear Call-to-Action (CTA)

End your ebook with a strong CTA that guides readers towards your upsell or next step in the customer journey.

Rule 8: Optimize for Skimmability

Use headers, bullet points, and short paragraphs to make your ebook easy to skim. Many readers will scan the content before deciding to read in-depth.

Rule 9: Provide Immediate, Actionable Value

Include at least one tip or strategy that readers can implement immediately. This quick win builds trust and keeps them engaged.

Rule 10: Make It Evergreen

While addressing current pain points, aim to create content that will remain relevant over time. This extends the life and usefulness of your lead magnet.

By following these rules, you'll create an ebook lead magnet that not only attracts potential customers but also sets the stage for a mutually beneficial relationship. Remember, the goal is to provide genuine value while strategically guiding readers toward your paid offerings.

3. Types of Content for Your Lead Magnet Ebook

When creating your ebook lead magnet, it's important to choose a content format that best suits your topic and audience. Here are three popular and effective types of content for ebooks, each with its own strengths:

1: Listicles

Listicles are articles structured as a list, making them easy to read and digest. They're perfect for providing quick, actionable information. Listicles are versatile and can cover a wide range of subtopics. Here are some specific approaches:

a) Examples:

- "10 Successful Email Marketing Campaigns (And Why They Worked)"
- "8 Case Studies of Startups That Pivoted to Success"
- "12 Before-and-After Home Staging Transformations"

b) Mistakes to Avoid:

- "7 Common Mistakes First-Time Home Buyers Make (And How to Avoid Them)"
- "9 Pitfalls to Watch Out for When Choosing a Web Host"
- "5 Critical Errors in Retirement Planning (And Their Solutions)"

c) How to Select a Reliable Vendor:

- "8 Key Criteria for Choosing the Right Digital Marketing Agency"
- "6 Essential Questions to Ask Before Hiring a Financial Advisor"
- "10 Red Flags to Watch for When Selecting a Dropshipping Supplier"

d) Tips and Tricks:

- "15 Little-Known Instagram Features to Boost Your Engagement"
- "7 Unconventional Networking Strategies That Actually Work"
- "12 Psychological Pricing Tactics to Increase Sales"

Why they work: Listicles offer variety and depth while remaining easy to digest. They provide clear value propositions and are highly shareable.

2: Cheat Sheets

Cheat sheets provide concise, practical information that readers can refer to repeatedly. They're excellent for technical or process-oriented topics.

Examples:

- "The Ultimate SEO Checklist for 2023"
- "Mastering Food Photography: A Pocket Guide"
- "30-Day Fitness Challenge Cheat Sheet"
- "Quick Reference: Essential Oil Blends for Common Ailments"
- "The Freelancer's Guide to Painless Invoicing"

Why they work: Cheat sheets offer immediate, actionable value and serve as go-to resources for your audience.

3: How to Guides

How-to guides provide step-by-step instructions for accomplishing a specific task or goal. They're ideal for demonstrating your expertise and providing clear value.

How-to guides can be structured in various ways to provide maximum value:

a) Step-by-Step Guides:

- "How to Set Up a Profitable Etsy Shop in 30 Days"
- "6 Steps to Mastering Public Speaking"
- "How to Create a Winning Business Plan: A Comprehensive Guide"
- "How to Launch Your First Podcast in 7 Days"
- "5 Steps to Creating a Thriving Organic Garden"
- "How to Build a Personal Brand on LinkedIn"
- "The Beginner's Guide to Mindfulness Meditation"
- "How to Plan a Budget-Friendly Wedding in 3 Months"

b) FAQ-Based Guides:

- "Your Top 20 Questions About Keto Diet Answered"
- "The Complete Guide to First-Time Home Buying: 25 FAQs Explained"
- "Understanding SEO: Answers to the 15 Most Common

Questions"

c) Myth-Busting Guides:

- "10 Fitness Myths Debunked: The Truth About Weight Loss"

- "7 Common Misconceptions About Stock Investing (And the Reality)"

- "The Truth Behind 8 Popular Marketing 'Rules' You've Been Told to Follow"

d) Insider Secrets:

- "5 Little-Known Tax Deductions Your Accountant Might Miss"

- "7 Insider Secrets Hotels Don't Want You to Know"

- "10 Hidden Features of [Popular Software] the Developers Don't Advertise"

Why they work: These guides directly address common pain points and curiosities, positioning you as an expert who can provide insider knowledge and clarify complex topics.

Additional Insights:

1. **Hybrid Approaches**: Don't be afraid to combine these

formats. For example, you could create a "10-Step Guide to [Topic], with Common Mistakes to Avoid at Each Stage."

2. **Data-Driven Content**: Incorporate statistics, survey results, or original research to add credibility to your ebook.

3. **Interactive Elements**: Consider adding quizzes, worksheets, or decision trees to engage readers and personalize the experience.

4. **Trend Analysis**: Offer predictions or analysis of upcoming trends in your industry to position yourself as a thought leader.

5. **Comparison Guides**: Create detailed comparisons of products, services, or methodologies in your field.

6. **Problem-Solution Format**: Structure your content around specific problems your audience faces and provide detailed solutions.

Choosing the Right Format

When deciding which format to use, consider:

1. Your audience's preferences and pain points

2. The complexity of your topic

3. The natural progression to your paid offering

4. Your brand voice and style

Remember, regardless of the format you choose, your ebook should provide clear value, be easy to consume, and leave your audience wanting more. This sets the stage for your upsell and helps build a lasting relationship with your readers.

4. Creating Your Ebook: A Step-by-Step Guide

Step 1. Choose Your Topic

Select a specific topic that addresses a pain point for your audience. For example, if you're a productivity coach, you might create "The 30-Day Focus Formula: Boost Your Productivity Without Burnout".

Step 2. Outline Your Content

Break your topic into manageable chapters. For our productivity ebook, it might look like:

- Chapter 1: Understanding Your Productivity Style

- Chapter 2: Setting Effective Goals

- Chapter 3: The Power of Time Blocking

- Chapter 4: Minimizing Distractions

- Chapter 5: The 30-Day Focus Plan

Step 3. Write Engaging Content

Use a conversational tone and include practical examples. For instance, in the chapter on time blocking, you could include a day-in-the-life example of a busy entrepreneur using this technique.

Step 4. Design Your Ebook

Use tools like Canva or Adobe InDesign to create an appealing layout. Include graphs, images, and infographics to break up text and illustrate key points.

Step 5. Add Interactive Elements

Consider including worksheets, checklists, or quizzes. In our productivity ebook, you could add a "Productivity Style Quiz" or a "Weekly Time Blocking Template".

Step 6. Create a Compelling Call-to-Action (CTA)

At the end of your ebook, include a clear next step for readers. This could be an invitation to join your email list, sign up for a free consultation, or explore your paid offerings.

5. Implementation Strategy

Step 1. Set Up a Landing Page

Create a dedicated page on your website for ebook downloads. Use compelling copy that highlights the benefits of your ebook.

Step 2. Create an Email Sequence

Develop a series of follow-up emails to engage readers after they download your ebook. For the productivity ebook, you could send tips expanding on each chapter over the course of a month.

Step 3. Promote Your Ebook

Share excerpts on social media, write blog posts on related topics, or guest post on relevant websites to drive traffic to your ebook landing page.

6. Example in Action

Ramit Sethi, personal finance expert, offers a free ebook called "Ultimate Guide to Personal Finance". He promotes it prominently on his website, uses it to capture email addresses, and follows up with a sequence of emails offering additional financial tips and promoting his paid courses.

Chapter 8: Crafting Captivating Online Courses

"Tell me and I forget. Teach me and I remember. Involve me and I learn." - Benjamin Franklin

In this chapter, we're exploring how to create engaging online courses that serve as powerful free gifts and lead magnets.

1. The Appeal of Online Courses

Free mini-courses can:

- Provide structured, high-value content
- Showcase your teaching style
- Build trust and credibility
- Naturally lead into your paid offerings

2. Creating Your Online Course: A Step-by-Step Guide

Step 1. Choose Your Course Topic

Select a specific skill or concept you can teach in a short timeframe. For example, if you're a social media marketer, you might create "5 Days to a Killer Instagram Strategy".

Step 2. Outline Your Modules

Break your course into bite-sized modules. For our Instagram course, it could look like:

- Day 1: Defining Your Instagram Aesthetic

- Day 2: Crafting Engaging Captions

- Day 3: Hashtag Strategy Mastery

- Day 4: Leveraging Instagram Stories

- Day 5: Building a Content Calendar

Step 3. Create Your Content

For each module, create:

- A short video lesson (5-10 minutes)

- A PDF summary of key points

- An actionable worksheet or assignment

Step 4. Set Up Your Course Platform

Use platforms like Teachable, Thinkific, or even a password-protected page on your website to host your course.

Step 5. Develop Engagement Strategies

Consider adding:

- Quizzes at the end of each module

- A private Facebook group for course takers

- Live Q&A sessions

Step 6. Create a Strong Completion Incentive

Offer a bonus for those who complete the course, such as a one-on-one strategy call or an exclusive webinar.

3. Implementation Strategy

Design an Attractive Course Landing Page

Highlight the benefits of your course, include testimonials if available, and make the sign-up process simple.

Develop an Email Nurture Sequence

Create emails that:

- Welcome students to the course

- Remind them of upcoming modules

- Encourage completion

- Offer your paid services as a natural next step

Promote Your Course

Use your email list, social media, and partnerships with other businesses to spread the word about your free course.

4. Example in Action

Digital Marketer offers a free mini-course called "Double Your Sales with Digital Marketing". It's prominently featured on their homepage, delivers high-value content over 5 days, and naturally leads into their more comprehensive paid training programs.

Chapter 9: Webinars and Free Talks: Engaging Your Audience Live

"The aim of marketing is to know and understand the customer so well the product or service fits him and sells itself." - Peter Druc

In this chapter, we're diving into the world of webinars and free talks - powerful tools for connecting with your audience in real-time.

1. The Power of Live Engagement

Webinars and free talks allow you to:

1. Build personal connections with your audience

2. Demonstrate your expertise in real-time

3. Address questions and concerns directly

4. Create a sense of exclusivity and urgency

2. Creating Your Webinar or Free Talk: A Step-by-Step Guide

Step 1. Choose Your Topic

Select a topic that addresses a specific pain point. For example, if you're a career coach, you might offer a webinar on "5 Proven Strategies to Ace Your Next Job Interview".

Step 2. Structure Your Content

Create an engaging structure, such as:

- Introduction and personal story (5 minutes)

- Overview of the 5 strategies (30 minutes)

- Live Q&A session (15 minutes)

- Special offer for attendees (5 minutes)

Step 3. Prepare Engaging Visuals

Create slides that enhance your talk, not just repeat what you're saying. Include relevant images, graphs, and key quotes.

Step 4. Plan Interactive Elements

Incorporate polls, chat questions, or even hot seat coaching to keep your audience engaged.

Step 5. Practice, Practice, Practice

Rehearse your presentation multiple times to ensure smooth delivery.

Step 6. Set Up Your Webinar Platform

Choose a platform like Zoom, WebinarJam, or GoToWebinar that suits your needs and budget.

3. Implementation Strategy

Step 1. Create a Compelling Registration Page

Highlight the benefits of attending, include a brief speaker bio, and make registration simple.

Step 2. Develop an Email Sequence

Create emails that:

- Confirm registration

- Remind attendees about the upcoming webinar

- Follow up with a replay link and special offer

Step 3. Promote Your Webinar

Use your email list, social media, paid ads, and partnerships to drive registrations.

Step 4. Repurpose Your Content

After the live event, turn your webinar into other types of content like blog posts, podcast episodes, or YouTube videos.

4. Example in Action

Marie Forleo frequently offers free training webinars that align with her B-School program. She promotes these heavily across her platforms, delivers high-value content during the webinar, and includes a time-sensitive offer for B-School at the end.

5. Making It Work: Webinars vs. Free Talks

Webinars are typically online and can reach a global audience. Free talks are usually in-person events that can create stronger local connections.

For webinars, focus on:

- Ensuring stable internet connection

- Using high-quality audio equipment

- Engaging with the chat function

For free talks, consider:

- Venue selection and logistics

- Body language and stage presence

- Handouts or physical materials

Remember, whether you're online or in-person, the key is to provide genuine value, engage your audience, and create a clear path to your paid offerings.

6. Action Items:

1. Choose one of these formats (ebook, online course, or webinar) to create in the next month.

2. Outline your chosen free gift, following the steps provided.

3. Set up the necessary tech tools (landing page, course platform, or webinar software).

7. Checklist:

[ ] Define your target audience for this free gift

[ ] Create a content outline

[ ] Develop your materials (writing, slides, or course content)

[ ] Set up the delivery method

[ ] Create a promotion plan

[ ] Develop a follow-up strategy to nurture leads

Remember, the key to success with any of these formats is to provide genuine value that leaves your audience wanting more. Good luck, and happy creating!

Chapter 10: Physical Pleasers: Leveraging Merchanise, Samples, Books, and Events to Wow

"The moment you make a mistake in pricing, you're eating into your reputation or your profits." - Katharine Paine

In this digital age, there's something special about physical gifts that can really make your brand stand out. Let's explore how to use tangible items and in-person experiences to create lasting impressions and foster deeper connections with your audience.

1. The Power of the Physical

While digital freebies are scalable and cost-effective, physical gifts offer unique advantages:

- **Tangibility**: People can touch, feel, and experience your brand in a concrete way.

- **Memorability**: Physical items serve as constant reminders of your brand.

- **Perceived Value**: Tangible gifts often feel more valuable than digital ones.

- **Personal Touch**: Physical gifts and events allow for more personal interactions.

Let's dive into three categories of physical pleasers:

2. Branded Merchandise

Merchandise, or promotional products, can turn your customers into walking billboards for your brand. But the key is to create items people actually want to use.

Tips for effective merchandise:

a) Choose useful items: Think beyond pens and keychains. Consider items like:

- High-quality water bottles

- Eco-friendly tote bags

- Portable phone chargers

- Comfortable t-shirts or hoodies

b) Prioritize quality: A well-made item will be used more and create a better impression.

c) Be creative with branding: Subtle, clever branding often works better than large logos.

d) Align with your brand values: If you're an eco-friendly company, choose sustainable merchandise.

Example in Action:

Patagonia, known for its environmental activism, gives away branded reusable utensil sets. This aligns perfectly with their brand values and provides practical value to their customers.

Implementation Strategy:

1. Identify your top customers or leads

2. Send them a surprise merchandise package

3. Include a personalized note explaining why you value them

4. Follow up with an email asking for feedback on the gift

3. Samples: Try Before You Buy

Samples allow potential customers to experience your product firsthand, reducing the perceived risk of purchase.

Tips for effective sampling:

a) Provide enough for a real experience: Don't be stingy with your samples.

b) Include clear instructions: Make it easy for people to use your sample correctly.

c) Follow up: Reach out after sending samples to gather feedback and offer special deals.

d) Consider "deluxe" samples: For higher-end products, create premium sample kits.

Example in Action:

Birchbox built an entire business model around product samples, partnering with beauty brands to send monthly sample boxes to subscribers.

Implementation Strategy:

1. Identify your most "sampleable" product

2. Create a sample request form on your website

3. Set up an automated email sequence for sample requesters

4. Include a special offer with each sample

4. Events: Creating Memorable Experiences

Events allow for face-to-face interactions and can create powerful emotional connections with your brand.

Types of events to consider:

a) Workshops or classes: Teach a skill related to your product or service.

b) Product launches: Create excitement around new offerings.

c) Appreciation events: Thank your best customers with exclusive gatherings.

d) Pop-up experiences: Create temporary, Instagram-worthy brand experiences.

Tips for successful events:

a) Provide real value: Ensure attendees learn something or have a unique experience.

b) Create photo opportunities: Design Instagram-worthy moments to encourage social sharing.

c) Offer exclusive perks: Give attendees special access or deals not available elsewhere.

d) Follow up: Send thank-you notes and gather feedback after the event.

Example in Action:

Lululemon regularly hosts free yoga classes in their stores and local parks. This aligns perfectly with their brand, provides value to their community, and naturally showcases their products.

Implementation Strategy:

1. Choose an event type that aligns with your brand and audience

2. Select a venue and set a date

3. Create an event landing page and registration process

4. Promote the event through email, social media, and partnerships

5. Plan engaging activities and valuable takeaways for attendees

5. Books as Physical Gifts

While we've discussed various types of physical pleasers, let's not overlook one of the most powerful: books. A physical book can be a highly effective marketing tool, as demonstrated by marketing legend Dan Kennedy.

Dan Kennedy, known for his "No B.S." book series, has masterfully used free book giveaways to attract high-quality leads. His strategy involves offering a physical copy of one of his books for free, with the recipient only paying for shipping and handling.

This approach accomplishes several key objectives:

1. Immediate Value: The recipient gets a tangible, valuable product.

2. Authority Positioning: Kennedy establishes himself as an expert in his field.

3. Direct Access: His message gets directly into the hands of potential clients.

4. Reciprocity: Recipients are more likely to engage with his paid offerings.

5. Differentiation: In a digital world, a physical book stands out.

Kennedy's strategy shows that even in our digital age, physical books can create a lasting impression and serve as powerful lead magnets.

Example:

Why Some Marketers Opt for Physical Books Only

Some marketers may choose to give away only physical books for several reasons:

1. **Tactile experience**: Physical books offer a sensory experience, and marketers may want to leverage this to create a memorable impression.

2. **Perceived value**: Physical books are often perceived as more valuable than ebooks, so marketers may use them as a premium offer.

3. **Exclusivity**: By only offering physical books, marketers may create a sense of exclusivity or scarcity, making the offer more appealing.

4. **Personal touch**: Signing and personalizing physical books can add a personal touch, making the gift more special.

5. **No digital distractions**: Physical books don't have hyperlinks or notifications, allowing readers to focus solely on the content

6. **Keep-sake**: Physical books can become a keepsake, sitting on a shelf or coffee table, serving as a constant reminder of the marketer's brand.

7. **Networking**: Physical books can be used as a networking tool, passed from person to person, potentially expanding the marketer's reach.

8. **Brand Positioning**: Offering only physical books can

position a brand as premium or traditionalist, which may align with certain marketing strategies.

9. **Longer Engagement**: Physical books may encourage longer engagement times compared to digital versions, potentially leading to better content retention.

10. **Gifting Potential**: Physical books are easier to gift to others, potentially extending the marketer's reach through secondary distribution.

11. **Event Marketing**: Physical books can be effectively used in event marketing, such as book signings or speaking engagements.

12. **Data Collection**: Shipping physical books requires address information, providing valuable data for future direct mail campaigns.

13. **Reduced Piracy**: Physical books are harder to duplicate and share illegally compared to digital versions.

14. **Complementary Material**: Physical books allow for the inclusion of additional materials like workbooks, CDs, or special inserts that enhance the overall package.

15. **Targeting Specific Demographics**: Some demographics, such as older generations or certain professional groups, may

prefer physical books, allowing for targeted marketing.

However, it's important to note that not offering an ebook version may limit the book's accessibility and reach, especially for international audiences or those who prefer digital content. A balanced approach, offering both ebook and physical book options, can help cater to different preferences and maximize the book's impact.

Implementing a Book Giveaway Strategy:

- Choose a book that showcases your expertise and provides real value.

- Set up a landing page offering the free book (plus shipping and handling).

- Use the book giveaway as a lead magnet in your marketing campaigns.

- Follow up with recipients to gather feedback and offer next steps.

6. Measuring Success

To ensure your physical pleasers are effective, track metrics such as:

- Usage rates of merchandise items

- Conversion rates from samples to purchases

- Event attendance and engagement levels

- Social media mentions and shares

- Customer feedback and testimonials

7. Balancing Physical and Digital

While physical pleasers can be powerful, they're often more expensive and less scalable than digital offerings. Consider using a mix of both:

- Offer digital freebies to a wide audience

- Reserve physical gifts for top customers or promising leads

- Use physical items to complement digital campaigns

8. Wrapping It Up

Physical pleasers offer a unique opportunity to create tangible connections with your audience. Whether it's a useful piece of merchandise, a generous product sample, or a memorable event, these tactile experiences can leave lasting impressions and foster deep brand loyalty.

Remember, the key is to provide genuine value and align these offerings with your overall brand strategy. When done right, physical pleasers can turn customers into devoted brand ambassadors.

9. Action Items:

1. Brainstorm 3-5 merchandise items that align with your brand and would be useful to your audience.

2. Plan a sampling campaign for one of your products.

3. Outline an event concept that would provide value to your customers.

10. Checklist:

[ ] Determine budget for physical marketing initiatives

[ ] Research suppliers for merchandise or samples

[ ] Create a distribution strategy for physical items

[ ] Develop a follow-up plan for after gifts are received or events are attended

[ ] Set up tracking systems to measure the impact of your physical pleasers

[ ] Plan how to integrate physical gifts with your digital marketing efforts

Remember, in a world increasingly dominated by digital experiences, physical pleasers can help your brand stand out and create meaningful, memorable connections with your audience. So go ahead, get creative, and start wowing your customers in the physical world!

Chapter 11: Experiential Extras: Creating Memorable Moments and Connections

People will forget what you said, people will forget what you did, but people will never forget how you made them feel." - Maya Angelou

In this chapter, we're going to explore how to create unforgettable experiences for your audience. In a world where consumers are increasingly valuing experiences over things, offering experiential extras can set your brand apart and create deep, lasting connections with your audience.

1. The Power of Experiences

Experiential marketing offers unique benefits:

- **Emotional Impact:** Experiences create stronger emotional ties to your brand.

- **Memorability**: People remember experiences more vividly than traditional advertising.

- **Shareable Moments:** Great experiences naturally encourage social sharing.

- **Personal Connections**: Face-to-face interactions build stronger relationships.

Let's dive into **different types of experiential extras:**

2. Interactive Workshops and Masterclasses

Workshops allow you to showcase your expertise while providing hands-on value to your audience.

Tips for successful workshops:

a) Focus on actionable skills: Ensure participants leave with practical knowledge.

b) Keep it interactive: Include exercises, group discussions, and Q&A sessions.

c) Provide take-home materials: Give participants resources to implement what they've learned.

d) Consider both in-person and virtual options: Cater to different preferences and reach a wider audience.

Example in Action:

Makeup brand Sephora offers free in-store makeup classes, allowing customers to learn techniques while trying products.

Implementation Strategy:

- Identify a key skill your audience wants to learn
- Develop a workshop curriculum
- Choose between in-person, virtual, or hybrid format
- Create engaging, hands-on activities
- Set up a registration system and promote the workshop

3. Behind-the-Scenes Tours

Offering exclusive looks into your operations can create a sense of insider access and deepen customer connections.

Tips for effective tours:

a) Showcase your unique processes or facilities

b) Introduce key team members

c) Include interactive elements or demonstrations

d) Offer exclusive insights or sneak peeks at upcoming products

Example in Action:

Ben & Jerry's factory tours in Vermont give visitors an inside look at ice cream production, complete with samples and a visit to the "Flavor Graveyard" of retired flavors.

Implementation Strategy:

- Identify interesting aspects of your business to showcase
- Develop a tour route and script
- Train staff to lead engaging tours
- Set up a booking system for tour slots
- Consider offering virtual tour options for remote audiences

4. Pop-Up Experiences

Temporary, immersive experiences can create buzz and offer unique brand interactions.

Tips for successful pop-ups:

a) Choose a strategic location with high foot traffic

b) Create an Instagram-worthy environment

c) Offer exclusive products or experiences

d) Limit the duration to create a sense of urgency

Example in Action:

Refinery29's "29Rooms" is an annual pop-up featuring interactive art installations, creating a highly shareable and immersive brand experience.

Implementation Strategy:

1. Conceptualize a unique, brand-aligned experience

2. Secure a suitable location

3. Design an eye-catching, interactive setup

4. Plan exclusive offerings or activities

5. Develop a promotional strategy to drive attendance

5. VIP Days or Retreats

Offering exclusive, high-value experiences for top customers or clients can foster deep loyalty and high-ticket sales.

Tips for impactful VIP experiences:

a) Limit attendance to create exclusivity

b) Offer personalized attention and customized content

c) Include luxury elements or unique venues

d) Provide opportunities for networking among participants

Example in Action:

Luxury car brand Porsche offers a "European Delivery" program where customers can pick up their new car at the factory in Germany and enjoy a curated driving experience through Europe.

Implementation Strategy:

- Define your ideal VIP client

- Design a high-value experience tailored to this audience

- Choose an appealing venue or destination

- Develop a detailed itinerary balancing learning, networking, and relaxation

- Create a selective application or invitation process

6. Virtual Reality (VR) or Augmented Reality (AR) Experiences

Leverage technology to create immersive brand experiences that can be accessed from anywhere.

Tips for effective VR/AR experiences:

a) Ensure the experience aligns closely with your brand or product

b) Make it easy to access and use

c) Create shareable moments within the experience

d) Offer something unique that can't be experienced in real life

Example in Action:

IKEA's AR app allows customers to virtually place furniture in their homes before purchasing, creating an interactive and practical brand experience.

Implementation Strategy:

1. Identify an aspect of your brand that could benefit from VR/AR

2. Partner with a tech company or hire developers to create the experience

3. Test thoroughly with your target audience

4. Develop a user guide or tutorial

5. Promote the experience across your marketing channels

7. Measuring Success

To ensure your experiential extras are effective, track metrics such as:

- Attendance or participation rates

- Social media mentions and shares

- Customer feedback and testimonials

- Sales or leads generated from the experience

- Repeat participation in future experiences

8. Balancing Cost and Impact

Experiential marketing can be more resource-intensive than traditional marketing. To maximize ROI:

- Start small and scale up based on success

- Repurpose content from experiences for other marketing channels

- Consider charging for premium experiences to offset costs

- Partner with complementary brands to share expenses and expand reach

9. Wrapping It Up

Experiential extras offer a powerful way to create memorable moments and deep connections with your audience. Whether it's an interactive workshop, an exclusive tour, a pop-up experience, a VIP retreat, or a cutting-edge VR experience, these initiatives can turn customers into true brand advocates.

Remember, the key is to align these experiences with your brand values and customer interests. When done right, experiential extras can create emotional bonds that last far beyond the experience itself.

10. Action Items:

- Brainstorm 3-5 experiential marketing ideas that align with your brand.

- Choose one idea and create a detailed implementation plan.

- Identify potential partners who could enhance or help execute your chosen experience.

11. Checklist:

[ ] Define clear objectives for your experiential marketing initiative

[ ] Identify your target audience for the experience

[ ] Develop a unique concept that aligns with your brand

[ ] Create a detailed budget and resource allocation plan

[ ] Design a promotional strategy to drive participation

[ ] Set up systems to capture feedback and measure success

[ ] Plan how to leverage the experience for ongoing marketing efforts

Remember, in a world of digital noise, creating real-world connections through memorable experiences can set your brand apart. So, get creative, think outside the box, and start crafting experiences that will wow your audience and keep them coming back for more!

Chapter 12: Crafting Compelling Offers: Writing Copy that Converts

"Make it simple. Make it memorable. Make it inviting to look at. Make it fun to read." - Leo Burnett

Welcome, wordsmith extraordinaire! In this chapter, we're going to explore the art and science of crafting irresistible offers and writing copy that turns readers into customers. Remember, even the most valuable free gift won't be effective if you can't communicate its worth. Let's dive in!

1. The Anatomy of a Compelling Offer

Before we get into the nitty-gritty of copywriting, let's break down what makes an offer truly compelling:

- Clear Value Proposition: What problem are you solving?

- Unique Selling Point (USP): Why is your solution better than alternatives?

- Risk Reversal: How are you removing barriers to saying "yes"?

- Scarcity/Urgency: Why should they act now?

Now, let's explore how to communicate these elements effectively.

2. The Art of Persuasive Copywriting

Step 1. Craft an Attention-Grabbing Headline

Your headline is your first (and sometimes only) chance to capture attention. Make it count!

Tips for effective headlines:

- Use power words that evoke emotion

- Include numbers or specific benefits

- Create curiosity or address a pain point

Example:

"Discover the 5-Minute Habit That Could Double Your Productivity (Free Guide)"

Step 2. Open with a Hook

Your opening paragraph should draw the reader in and make them want to keep reading.

Techniques for a strong hook:

- Ask a thought-provoking question

- Share a surprising statistic

- Tell a relatable story

Example:

"What if I told you that the most productive people in the world all share one simple habit? And what if you could learn this habit in just 5 minutes a day?"

Step 3. Highlight Benefits, Not Just Features

People don't buy products or services; they buy outcomes. Focus on how your offer will improve their lives.

Try this exercise:

List all the features of your offer, then ask "So what?" for each one to uncover the true benefits.

Example:

Feature: "30-page ebook"

Benefit: "Discover a proven system to reclaim hours of your day and achieve more without burning out"

Step 4. Use the Problem-Agitate-Solve (PAS) Formula

This classic copywriting formula works wonders:

- Identify a problem your audience faces

- Agitate that problem by highlighting its negative impacts

- Present your offer as the solution

Example:

"Feeling overwhelmed by your never-ending to-do list? (Problem)

Each day, it seems like you're falling further behind, missing deadlines and disappointing others - not to mention yourself. (Agitate)

But what if there was a simple system to take control of your time and skyrocket your productivity? (Solve)"

Step 5. Incorporate Social Proof

People trust the opinions of others. Use testimonials, case studies, or statistics to build credibility.

Example:

"Join over 10,000 professionals who have transformed their productivity with this free guide"

Step 6. Create a Sense of Urgency or Scarcity

Encourage immediate action by highlighting limited availability or time-sensitive bonuses.

Example:

"The first 100 people to download the guide will also receive a free 30-minute productivity coaching call (Value: $97)"

Step 7. Use Clear, Compelling Calls-to-Action (CTAs)

Tell your readers exactly what to do next, and make it easy for them to do it.

Tips for effective CTAs:

- Use action-oriented language

- Create a sense of immediacy

- Make them stand out visually

Example:

"Click Here to Download Your Free Productivity Guide Now!"

Step 8. Address Objections Preemptively

Anticipate potential concerns and address them in your copy.

Example:

"No time to read a long ebook? Don't worry - our guide is designed for busy professionals and can be consumed in bite-sized chunks."

3. Putting It All Together: A Template for Your Offer

Here's a basic structure you can follow:

1. Attention-Grabbing Headline

2. Opening Hook

3. Problem-Agitate-Solve (PAS)

4. Clear Value Proposition

5. Benefits (not just features)

6. Social Proof

7. Overcome Objections

8. Urgency/Scarcity

9. Clear Call-to-Action

Example:

Headline: "Unlock the Secret to 10x Productivity with Our Free 5-Minute Habit Guide"

Hook: "What if the key to transforming your productivity was just 5 minutes away?"

PAS: "In today's fast-paced world, it's easy to feel overwhelmed and under-productive. You're constantly juggling tasks, missing deadlines, and watching your to-do list grow longer each day. But what if there was a simple solution?"

Value Proposition: "Introducing the '5-Minute Productivity Hack' - a free guide that reveals the one habit shared by the world's most successful people."

Benefits: "In this guide, you'll discover:

- How to reclaim hours of your day with one simple technique

- The psychology behind this powerful habit (and why it works for everyone)

- A step-by-step system to implement this habit in your life immediately"

Social Proof: "Join over 10,000 professionals who have already transformed their productivity with this guide"

Overcome Objections: "No time for complex systems? Don't worry - this habit takes just 5 minutes a day to implement."

Urgency: "Download now and get a bonus '30-Day Productivity Planner' (Limited to the first 100 downloads)"

CTA: "Click Here to Download Your Free Guide and Start Boosting Your Productivity Today!"

4. Wrapping It Up

Crafting compelling offers and writing persuasive copy is both an art and a science. It requires understanding your audience, clearly communicating value, and motivating action. With practice and testing, you'll find the right formula that resonates with your audience and converts readers into eager participants.

5. Action Items:

- Review the copy for your current free offer using the template provided
- Rewrite your offer headline using at least three different techniques

- Gather testimonials or data to incorporate as social proof in your copy

6. Checklist:

[ ] Clearly define the value proposition of your offer

[ ] Craft an attention-grabbing headline

[ ] Use the PAS formula to structure your copy

[ ] Highlight benefits, not just features

[ ] Incorporate relevant social proof

[ ] Address potential objections

[ ] Create a sense of urgency or scarcity

[ ] Include clear, compelling calls-to-action

Remember, great copy isn't about tricks or gimmicks - it's about clearly communicating the genuine value you're offering. Keep refining your message, testing different approaches, and always focus on how you can truly help your audience. Happy writing!

Chapter 13: Delivering Delight: Ensuring a Seamless Customer Experience

"Your most unhappy customers are your greatest source of learning." - Bill Gate

In this chapter, we're going to explore how to create a seamless, delightful experience for your customers when they receive your free gift. Remember, the way you deliver your freebie can be just as important as the gift itself. Let's dive in!

1. The Importance of a Seamless Experience

A smooth, enjoyable experience when receiving your free gift can:

- Reinforce the value of your offering
- Build trust and credibility for your brand

- Increase the likelihood of further engagement

- Encourage word-of-mouth recommendations

Let's break down the key elements of delivering delight:

2. Set Clear Expectations

From the moment someone signs up for your free gift, they should know exactly what to expect.

Tips for setting expectations:

- Clearly communicate what they'll receive and when

- Explain any steps they need to take

- Provide an estimated timeframe for delivery

Example:

"Thank you for requesting our 'Productivity Powerhouse' ebook! Here's what happens next:

- Check your email in the next 5 minutes for your download link

- Click the link to access your ebook instantly

- Look out for a follow-up email tomorrow with bonus tips!"

3. Streamline the Delivery Process

Make it as easy as possible for people to access your free gift.

Tips for streamlined delivery:

- Minimize the number of clicks required

- Ensure your download or access page loads quickly

- Make your gift accessible on multiple devices

Example:

For a free ebook, instead of requiring people to create an account, simply email them a direct download link that works on both desktop and mobile.

4. Create a Welcoming Experience

First impressions matter. Make people feel valued from the moment they receive your gift.

Ideas for a welcoming experience:

- Include a personalized welcome message

- Provide a quick-start guide or overview

- Offer a video introduction from you

Example:

"Welcome, [Name]! We're thrilled you've joined our Productivity Powerhouse community. To help you get started, we've created this 2-minute video introduction. Click here to watch!"

5. Anticipate and Address Potential Issues

Think about what might go wrong and proactively address these issues.

Tips for issue prevention:

- Provide FAQs or troubleshooting guides

- Offer multiple ways to access the gift (e.g., direct download and cloud storage link)

- Set up automated systems to resend access if needed

Example:

"Didn't receive your download link? No problem! Click here to have it resent instantly. If you're still having trouble, check out our FAQ page or contact our support team."

6. Follow Up and Provide Additional Value

Don't let the relationship end once they've received the gift. Follow up to ensure they're getting value and offer additional resources.

Ideas for follow-up:

- Send a sequence of emails with tips on how to best use your gift
- Offer complementary resources or bonus content
- Ask for feedback and suggestions

Example:

"Hey [Name], it's been a week since you downloaded our Productivity Powerhouse ebook. How's it going? We'd love to hear about any 'aha' moments you've had. Reply to this email and let us know!"

7. Make it Easy to Share

If people love your free gift, make it easy for them to tell others about it.

Tips for encouraging sharing:

- Include social sharing buttons

- Offer an incentive for referrals

- Provide pre-written social media posts they can use

Example:

"Loving the Productivity Powerhouse ebook? Share it with your friends! For every friend who downloads, we'll send you an exclusive productivity hack. Click here to share now!"

8. Ensure Consistent Branding

Your free gift should feel like a seamless extension of your brand.

Tips for consistent branding:

- Use consistent colors, fonts, and imagery

- Maintain your brand voice across all touchpoints

- Ensure your gift aligns with your overall brand promise

Example:

If your brand is known for a fun, casual tone, make sure this comes through in everything from your download page to your follow-up emails.

9. Gather and Act on Feedback

Continuously improve your delivery process by actively seeking and acting on feedback.

Ideas for gathering feedback:

- Send a short survey after delivery

- Monitor social media mentions

- Analyze user behavior (e.g., download rates, engagement with follow-up emails)

Example:

"We hope you're enjoying the Productivity Powerhouse ebook! We'd love to know how we can make it even better. Could you take 2 minutes to answer 3 quick questions? Your input helps us serve you better!"

10. Go Above and Beyond

Look for opportunities to surprise and delight your audience beyond their expectations.

Ideas for exceeding expectations:

- Offer unexpected bonus content

- Provide personal, non-automated responses when possible

- Celebrate milestones or achievements

Example:

"Congratulations on completing the 30-day Productivity Challenge! As a special thank you, we've unlocked an exclusive bonus chapter in your ebook. Check it out now!"

11. Putting It All Together: A Seamless Experience Roadmap

Here's a basic flow you can follow:

1. Clear, enticing offer
2. Easy sign-up process
3. Immediate confirmation with clear next steps
4. Quick, hassle-free delivery of the gift
5. Welcoming message and quick-start guide
6. Follow-up sequence with additional value
7. Request for feedback
8. Encouragement to share
9. Surprise bonus or recognition

12. Wrapping It Up

Delivering delight is about more than just providing a valuable free gift – it's about creating a seamless, enjoyable experience from start to finish. By setting clear expectations, streamlining delivery, anticipating issues, following up with value, and going above and beyond, you can turn a simple freebie into a powerful tool for building lasting relationships with your audience.

13. Action Items:

- Map out the current journey for someone receiving your free gift
- Identify at least three areas where you can improve the experience
- Create a follow-up email sequence to provide additional value after gift delivery

14. Checklist:

[ ] Audit your current delivery process for potential friction points

[ ] Ensure all branding is consistent across touchpoints

[ ] Set up a system for gathering and acting on feedback

[ ] Create FAQs or troubleshooting resources

[ ] Develop a plan for surprising and delighting recipients

[ ] Test your delivery process on multiple devices

[ ] Set up tracking to monitor engagement and identify areas for improvement

Remember, the way you deliver your free gift is a reflection of your brand and a preview of what it's like to work with you. By focusing on creating a seamless, delightful experience, you're not just giving away a freebie – you're building relationships, trust, and loyalty that can lead to long-term success. Happy delivering!

Chapter 14: Measuring Success: Tracking the Impact of Your Free Gifts

What gets measured gets managed." - Peter Drucker

In this chapter, we're going to explore how to measure the success of your free gift strategy. After all, as the management guru Peter Drucker famously said, "If you can't measure it, you can't improve it." Let's dive into the world of metrics and analytics to ensure your free gifts are truly moving the needle for your business.

1. Why Measurement Matters

Tracking the impact of your free gifts allows you to:

- Understand what's working and what's not

- Justify the resources invested in creating and distributing free gifts

- Continuously improve your strategy

- Make data-driven decisions about future offerings

2. Key Metrics to Track

Let's break down the essential metrics you should be monitoring:

1. Acquisition Metrics

These metrics help you understand how effectively you're attracting people to your free gift.

- Opt-in Rate: The percentage of visitors who sign up for your free gift

- Cost Per Lead (CPL): If you're using paid advertising, how much does each new lead cost?

- Traffic Sources: Where are your sign-ups coming from?

Example:

If you're offering a free ebook on your website, you might find that your opt-in rate is 5% (5 out of every 100 visitors sign up), your CPL is $2 if you're using Facebook ads, and 60% of your sign-ups come from organic search traffic.

2. Engagement Metrics

These metrics show you how people are interacting with your free gift.

- Download/Consumption Rate: What percentage of people who sign up actually download or use your free gift?

- Completion Rate: For multi-part gifts (like email courses), what percentage of people complete the entire offering?

- Time Spent: How long do people spend engaging with your gift?

Example:

For a 5-day email course, you might find that 80% of subscribers open the first email, 60% complete the entire course, and on average, people spend 10 minutes reading each email.

3. Sharing Metrics

These metrics indicate how viral your free gift is becoming.

- Social Shares: How often is your free gift being shared on social media?

- Referral Rate: What percentage of new sign-ups come from

referrals?

Example:

You might discover that your free productivity planner gets shared on average 3 times for every 10 downloads, and 15% of your new sign-ups come from referrals.

4. Follow-up Engagement Metrics

These metrics help you understand how your free gift is impacting ongoing engagement with your brand.

- Email Open Rates: Are people who downloaded your free gift more likely to open your subsequent emails?

- Click-Through Rates: Do they click on links in your emails more often?

- Website Return Rate: Do they come back to your website more frequently?

Example:

You might find that people who downloaded your free ebook have a 10% higher email open rate and visit your website twice as often as those who haven't.

5. Conversion Metrics

Ultimately, you want to know if your free gift is leading to paid conversions.

- Lead-to-Customer Conversion Rate: What percentage of people who download your free gift eventually become paying customers?

- Customer Lifetime Value (CLV): Do customers who started with your free gift tend to spend more over time?

- Sales Cycle Length: Does your free gift shorten the time it takes for someone to become a customer?

Example:

You might discover that 5% of people who download your free guide eventually enroll in your paid course, compared to only 1% of those who don't download the guide. Additionally, these customers might have a 20% higher CLV.

3. Tools for Tracking

To gather these metrics, you'll need some tools in your arsenal:

- Google Analytics: For website traffic, behavior, and conversion tracking

- Email Marketing Software: Most platforms (like MailChimp or ConvertKit) offer detailed engagement analytics

- Social Media Analytics: To track shares and engagement on social platforms

- CRM Software: To track lead-to-customer conversions and customer lifetime value

- Survey Tools: To gather qualitative feedback from your audience

4. Setting Up Your Tracking System

Here's a step-by-step guide to set up your measurement system:

1. **Identify Your Key Performance Indicators (KPIs):** Based on your business goals, decide which metrics matter most to you.

2. **Set Up Tracking**: Ensure you have the necessary tools and tracking codes in place.

3. **Establish Baselines**: Measure your current performance to have a point of comparison.

4. **Set Goals:** Determine what success looks like for each

metric.

5. **Create a Reporting Schedule**: Decide how often you'll review your metrics (weekly, monthly, quarterly).

6. **Analyze and Adjust**: Regularly review your data and make informed decisions based on what you learn.

5. Interpreting Your Data

Remember, numbers alone don't tell the whole story. Here are some tips for interpreting your data:

1. **Look for Trends:** Don't fixate on day-to-day fluctuations. Look for patterns over time.

2. **Compare Metrics**: Often, the relationship between metrics can provide deeper insights than any single metric.

3. **Consider Context**: External factors (like seasonal changes or market conditions) can impact your metrics.

4. **Gather Qualitative Data**: Use surveys or interviews to understand the "why" behind the numbers.

5. **Test and Learn**: Use A/B testing to experiment with different approaches and see what works best.

6. Wrapping It Up

Measuring the success of your free gifts is crucial for optimizing your strategy and maximizing your return on investment. By tracking the right metrics, using appropriate tools, and regularly analyzing your data, you can ensure that your free gifts are truly making an impact on your business goals.

Remember, the goal isn't just to collect data, but to gain insights that drive action. Use what you learn to continuously refine your free gift strategy, improve the user experience, and ultimately, grow your business.

7. Action Items:

- Identify the top 5 metrics that are most important for your business goals

- Set up tracking for these metrics if you haven't already

- Establish a regular schedule for reviewing and analyzing your data

8. Checklist:

[ ] Define your key performance indicators (KPIs)

[ ] Set up necessary tracking tools and codes

[ ] Establish baseline measurements for each KPI

[ ] Set specific, measurable goals for each metric

[ ] Create a reporting template or dashboard for easy data review

[ ] Schedule regular data review sessions

[ ] Develop a system for acting on insights gained from your data

Remember, what gets measured gets managed. By tracking the impact of your free gifts, you're not just giving away value – you're strategically growing your business. Happy measuring!

Chapter 15: The Art of the Upsell: Turning Free Gifts into Profitable Relationships

"The sale begins when the customer says yes." ~ Harvey Mackay, bestselling author and business motivational speaker

1. Introduction: The Free Gift to Paid Offer Pipeline

In the world of digital marketing, free gifts serve as powerful tools to attract and engage potential customers. However, their true power lies in their ability to pave the way for paid offerings. This chapter explores how to effectively transition from providing free value to securing profitable customer relationships through strategic upsells.

The purpose of free gifts in the marketing funnel

Free gifts, or lead magnets, are designed to attract potential customers by providing immediate value. They serve as the first step in building a relationship with your audience, demonstrating your expertise and the quality of your offerings.

The 50/50 principle: Free gifts as half the solution

A well-crafted free gift should provide approximately 50% of the solution to your audience's problem. It typically covers the '**Why**' (why the problem exists or why it needs to be solved) and the '**What**' (what needs to be done to solve it). This approach creates value while leaving room for your paid offering to provide the crucial '**How**' - the detailed implementation steps.

2. Understanding the Upsell

Definition and importance of upsells

An upsell is a sales technique where a seller induces the customer to purchase more expensive items, upgrades, or other add-ons to generate more revenue. In the context of free gifts, upsells are the natural next step, offering a more comprehensive solution to the customer's problem.

How upsells complement free gifts

While free gifts provide valuable information and build trust, upsells offer the complete solution. They bridge the gap between the customer's newfound knowledge (from the free gift) and the actual implementation of the solution.

The psychology behind effective upsells

Effective upsells leverage principles of reciprocity, commitment, and consistency. Having received value from the free gift, customers are more likely to feel obligated to reciprocate by considering your paid offer. Additionally, they've already committed to solving their problem by engaging with your free content, making them more likely to follow through with a purchase.

3. Crafting the Perfect Upsell

Aligning your upsell with your free gift

Your upsell should be a natural extension of your free gift. It should promise to build upon the knowledge gained from the free content and offer a more in-depth, actionable solution.

Creating a seamless transition from free to paid

The transition from free to paid should feel logical and valuable to the customer. Use language that emphasizes how the paid offering completes the picture presented in the free gift.

Pricing strategies for upsells

Consider tiered pricing options or payment plans to make your upsell more accessible. The perceived value of your upsell should significantly outweigh its cost.

4. The 'Why', 'What', and 'How' Framework

Free gifts: Delivering the 'Why' and 'What'

Your free gift should clearly explain why the problem needs solving and what general steps are involved in the solution. This creates a foundation of understanding and motivates the customer to seek more detailed guidance.

Upsells: Providing the crucial 'How'

Your paid offer should provide detailed, step-by-step instructions on how to implement the solution. This might include specific strategies, tools, templates, or personalized guidance.

Case studies of successful 'Why-What-How' implementations

(Include 2-3 brief case studies of businesses successfully using this framework)

5. Timing Your Upsell

Immediate vs. delayed upsells

Decide whether to offer your upsell immediately after the free gift is accessed, or to nurture the lead over time before presenting the offer. Both approaches can be effective depending on your audience and offer.

Creating urgency without pressure

Use scarcity tactics (limited time offers, limited spots available) to create urgency, but avoid high-pressure sales tactics that could damage trust.

The role of follow-up sequences in upselling

Develop an email sequence that provides additional value while subtly leading towards your upsell offer.

6. Crafting Compelling Upsell Offers

Tips:

- **Value proposition: Why they need the 'How'.** Clearly articulate why the 'How' is crucial for success and how your paid offering provides this missing piece.

- **Overcoming objections in your upsell pitch.** Anticipate common objections (price, time commitment, etc.) and address them proactively in your upsell messaging.

- **Using scarcity and exclusivity effectively.** Highlight any limited-time bonuses or exclusive elements of your paid offer to increase its perceived value.

Simple Upsell Template:

1. **Acknowledge and Congratulate**

   - Thank them for downloading the lead magnet

   - Briefly reinforce the value they'll get from it

2. **Identify the Gap**

- Highlight what the lead magnet doesn't cover
- Introduce a bigger problem or goal

3. **Present the Solution**

    - Introduce your paid offer as the complete solution
    - Emphasize how it builds on the lead magnet

4. **Highlight Key Benefits**

    - List 3-5 main benefits of your paid offer
    - Focus on outcomes, not features

5. **Provide Social Proof**

    - Share 1-2 brief testimonials or results

6. **Make the Offer**

    - Clearly state what they'll get
    - Mention any time-sensitive or exclusive elements

7. **Call to Action**

    - Use clear, action-oriented language
    - Reiterate the main benefit

Here's how it might look in practice:

Thanks for downloading [Lead Magnet]! You're on your way to [Small Win].

While [Lead Magnet] gives you a great start, it doesn't cover [Bigger Goal]. That's where many people get stuck.

Introducing [Paid Offer], the complete system for [Achieving Bigger Goal]. It takes everything you learned in [Lead Magnet] and shows you exactly how to implement it for maximum results.

With [Paid Offer], you'll:

- [Benefit 1]
- [Benefit 2]
- [Benefit 3]

Just ask [Customer Name], who [Achieved Result] in just [Time Frame].

For a limited time, you can get [Paid Offer] for just [Price]. It includes [List of Components].

Ready to [Achieve Bigger Goal]? Click here to get started now!

Example:

Here's a real example of an upsell using the simplified template. Let's assume we're selling a comprehensive course on digital marketing after offering a free ebook on social media basics.

Thanks for downloading "10 Social Media Hacks for Beginners"! You're on your way to boosting your online presence.

While these hacks will definitely improve your social media game, they don't cover the full spectrum of digital marketing. That's where many small businesses struggle to grow.

Introducing "Digital Marketing Mastery," the complete system for transforming your online presence and skyrocketing your sales. It takes everything you learned in the social media guide and shows you exactly how to integrate it into a comprehensive digital marketing strategy.

With "Digital Marketing Mastery," you'll:

- Create a cohesive online brand that attracts your ideal customers

- Master SEO techniques that bring organic traffic to your website

- Develop email marketing campaigns that convert leads into loyal customers

Just ask Sarah, owner of Bloom Boutique, who tripled her online sales in just 3 months after implementing our strategies.

For the next 48 hours, you can get "Digital Marketing Mastery" for just $297 (regular price $497). It includes 6 in-depth modules, weekly live Q&A sessions, and a private community of fellow entrepreneurs.

Ready to take your business to the next level? Click here to enroll in Digital Marketing Mastery now!

This example:

1. Acknowledges the free ebook they've downloaded

2. Identifies a larger need (comprehensive digital marketing)

3. Introduces the paid course as a solution

4. Highlights key benefits

5. Provides a specific customer success story

6. Makes a time-limited offer with clear components

7. Ends with a strong call to action

This upsell naturally builds on the free lead magnet, addressing a broader need that the target audience (small business owners interested in improving their online presence) likely has. It's concise yet compelling, hitting all the key points that motivate a purchase decision.

7. Testing and Optimizing Your Upsell Strategy

Key metrics to track

Monitor conversion rates, average order value, and customer lifetime value to assess the effectiveness of your upsell strategy.

A/B testing your upsell offers

Continuously test different aspects of your upsell (pricing, timing, messaging) to optimize performance.

Continual refinement of your upsell process

Use data and customer feedback to continually improve your upsell strategy.

8. Ethical Considerations in Upselling

Maintaining trust while pursuing sales

Always prioritize providing genuine value over making a quick sale. Your upsell should truly benefit the customer.

Ensuring your upsell truly provides value

Your paid offering should deliver on its promises and provide significant additional value beyond the free gift.

Handling customers who decline the upsell

Continue to provide value and maintain a positive relationship with all customers, regardless of whether they purchase your upsell.

9. Integrating Upsells into Your Overall Marketing Strategy

Upsells as part of your customer journey map

View upsells as a key stage in your overall customer journey, not just a one-time sales opportunity.

Balancing free content and paid offerings

Strike a balance between providing free value and monetizing your expertise. Your free content should be valuable in its own right, while still leaving room for paid offerings.

Building a sustainable business model with smart upselling

Use upsells to create a sustainable revenue stream that allows you to continue providing high-quality free content.

Remember, the key to successful upselling lies in genuinely serving your audience. When done right, upsells benefit both your business and your customers, creating a win-win situation that fosters long-term, mutually beneficial relationships.

Conclusion: The Gift that Keeps on Giving: Sustaining a Culture of Generosity

"No one has ever become poor by giving." - Anne Frank

Congratulations! You've made it to the end of our journey through the art of giving. By now, you should have a solid understanding of how free gifts can transform your business, win customers' hearts, and drive sustainable growth. But as we conclude, let's zoom out and consider the bigger picture: creating a lasting culture of generosity in your business.

1. The Ripple Effect of Generosity

When you embrace the practice of giving, you're not just implementing a marketing tactic – you're fostering a mindset that can permeate every aspect of your business. This culture of generosity can:

- **Attract Like-Minded Customers**: People are drawn to brands that align with their values. By prioritizing generosity, you'll naturally attract customers who appreciate and reciprocate that mindset.

- **Inspire Employee Engagement**: When your team sees the positive impact of your generous initiatives, they're likely to feel more connected to your mission and motivated in their work.

- **Encourage Innovation**: A giving mindset often leads to creative thinking about how to provide more value, spurring innovation in your products and services.

- **Build a Supportive Community**: Generosity breeds generosity. As you give freely to your audience, you'll likely find them more willing to support you and each other.

- **Create Lasting Relationships**: The connections formed through genuine generosity tend to be stronger and more enduring than those based solely on transactions.

2. Sustaining Your Giving Strategy

To maintain a culture of generosity over the long term:

- **Make it a Core Value**: Integrate generosity into your company's mission and values. Let it guide decision-making at all levels.

- **Lead by Example**: As a leader, consistently demonstrate generosity in your interactions with customers, employees, and partners.

- **Celebrate Generosity**: Recognize and reward acts of generosity within your organization and community.

- **Continuously Innovate**: Regularly brainstorm new ways to provide value to your audience. What worked yesterday may not be enough tomorrow.

- **Listen to Your Audience**: Stay attuned to your customers' evolving needs and desires. Let their feedback guide your giving strategy.

- **Balance Generosity and Sustainability**: Ensure your giving initiatives are sustainable for your business. It's okay to say no sometimes or to adjust your approach as needed.

- **Measure and Refine**: Regularly assess the impact of your giving initiatives and be willing to refine your approach based on data and feedback.

3. The Transformative Power of Giving

As we've explored throughout this book, the impact of strategic giving goes far beyond immediate marketing gains. It has the power to:

- Transform your relationship with your audience from transactional to relational

- Differentiate your brand in a crowded marketplace

- Create a positive feedback loop of goodwill and growth

- Align your business practices with your personal values

- Contribute positively to your industry and community

Remember, at its core, business is about creating value for others. By embracing a culture of generosity, you're not just growing your business – you're maximizing your positive impact on the world.

4. Final Thoughts

As you move forward with your giving strategy, remember that authenticity is key. Your audience can sense when your generosity is genuine and when it's merely a marketing ploy. Stay true to your values, focus on providing real value, and trust that the benefits will follow.

The journey of generosity is ongoing. There will always be new ways to give, new needs to meet, and new connections to forge. Embrace this journey with an open heart and an innovative mind.

Thank you for joining me on this exploration of "The Art of Giving: How Free Gifts Can Win Customers' Hearts." I hope you feel inspired and equipped to implement a powerful giving strategy in your business. Remember, every act of generosity, no matter how small, has the potential to create a ripple effect of positivity.

Now, go forth and give generously. Your customers, your business, and the world at large will be better for it.

5. Action Items:

- Reflect on your current business practices. Where can you integrate more generosity?

- Draft a generosity mission statement for your business.

- Plan your next free gift, keeping in mind the principles we've discussed.

6. Final Checklist:

[ ] Review and update your company values to reflect a commitment to generosity

[ ] Schedule regular team discussions about new giving initiatives

[ ] Set up a system for gathering and acting on customer feedback

[ ] Plan how you'll measure and report on the impact of your giving strategy

[ ] Identify potential partners or collaborators for future giving initiatives

[ ] Create a content calendar that includes regular free value for your audience

[ ] Commit to personal acts of generosity in your professional network

Remember, in the world of business, generosity is not just a nice-to-have – it's a powerful strategy for growth, connection, and lasting success. Here's to your journey of generous marketing and the amazing results it will bring!

www.ingramcontent.com/pod-product-compliance
Lightning Source LLC
Chambersburg PA
CBHW052159220526
45471CB00004B/1732